Teaching Physical Education to Children with Special Educational Needs

One in five children in England and Wales is now identified as having an SEN, and consequently teachers of PE are facing daily challenges to facilitate pupils' accessibility and entitlement to inclusion within mainstream school contexts.

Offering a combination of theoretical and practical strategies to include children with SEN within lessons, this unique title:

- directly applies current research to the practice of including children with SEN in PE;
- offers an outline of the statutory responsibilities placed upon teachers and schools to include children with SEN in PE;
- covers a diverse range of issues, which teachers need to address in order to provide high quality learning experiences for children with SEN;
- includes a series of reflective tasks, extended reading and further contacts within each chapter to assist with the development of knowledge and understanding of SEN and PE.

This authoritative book offers an opportunity to explore in depth the complexities of including children with SEN in PE. This is an extensive resource that requires no prior knowledge of the topic and is essential reading for practitioners who want to involve *all* children in physical activities and education.

Philip Vickerman is at Liverpool John Moores University, UK.

Teaching Physical Education to Children with Special Educational Needs

Philip Vickerman

Routledge
Taylor & Francis Group

LONDON AND NEW YORK

First published 2007
by Routledge
2 Park Square, Milton Park, Abingdon, Oxon OX14 4RN

Simultaneouly published in the USA and Canada
by Routledge
270 Madison Ave, New York NY 10016

Routledge is an imprint of the Taylor & Francis Group, an informa business

Typeset in Garamond and Gill by BC Typesetting Ltd, Bristol
Printed and bound in Great Britain by
TJ International Ltd., Padstow, Cornwall

British Library Cataloguing in Publication Data
A catalogue record for this book is available from the British Library

Library of Congress Cataloging in Publication Data
Vickerman, Philip, 1968–
    Teaching Physical Education to Children with Special Educational Needs/
    Philip Vickerman
        p. cm.
    Includes bibliographical references.
    ISBN 0–415–38949–6 (hbk) – ISBN 0–415–38950–X (pbk).
    1. Physical Education for Children with Disabilities – Great Britain.
    I. Title. GV245.V53 2007
    371.9′04486–dc22   2006015991

ISBN10: 0–415–38949–6 (hbk)
ISBN10: 0–415–38950–X (pbk)
ISBN10: 0–203–96811–5 (ebk)

ISBN13: 978–0–415–38949–5 (hbk)
ISBN13: 978–0–415–38950–1 (pbk)
ISBN13: 978–0–203–96811–6 (ebk)

This book is dedicated to my wife Heather, and children
Liam and Hannah

Contents

Tasks

Preface

This book has been written as a resource to assist trainee teachers, practitioners and those in leadership, advisory or lecturing positions to reflect upon their knowledge and understanding of including children with special educational needs (SEN) in physical education (PE). There is significant evidence that more and more children with SEN are either entering mainstream schools or wanting more access to PE.

This book combines aspects of theory, research, reflective tasks, further reading and practice-based evidence within a context of encouraging the reader to critically review their existing strategies for engaging with children with SEN in PE. The book is structured around themed chapters which offer a combination of theory, practical guidance, reflective tasks and further reading. It is hoped that through this approach the book will cater for a diverse range of individuals' needs in developing a wide appreciation of all the pertinent issues related to inclusive PE.

This book can be used as a guide for trainee teachers to develop their knowledge, whilst using the reflective tasks to assist with gathering evidence against the Qualified Teacher Status (QTS) Standards. Furthermore, trainee teachers could use these tasks with mentors when on school-based experience to act as points for discussion and clarity. In addition, the book will be of use to experienced practitioners and those in leadership roles as it offers theoretical underpinning and research evidence to review many of the points made.

I hope you find this book helpful to you in gaining a wider appreciation of the issues that surround the inclusion of children with SEN in PE with the key emphasis being a desire to be flexible, have high expectations of individuals and be prepared to modify your practices in order to maximise successful learning and participation.

Abbreviations

ADHD	Attention deficit hyperactivity disorder
BAALPE	British Association of Advisers and Lecturers in Physical Education
CPD	Continuing professional development
DCD	Development Co-ordination Disorder
DCMS	Department for Culture, Media and Sport
DES	Department of Education and Science
DoE	Department of Education
DfEE	Department for Education and Employment
DfES	Department for Education and Skills
DH	Department of Health
EAL	English as an additional language
EFDS	English Federation for Disability Sport
IEP	Individual education plan
ITT	Initial teacher training
LEA	Local education authority
NC	National Curriculum
NDSO	National disability sport organisation
NQT	Newly qualified teacher
OFSTED	Office for Standards in Education
PE	Physical education
PEA (UK)	Physical Education Association (United Kingdom)
PESSCL	PE, School Sport and Club Links
PCE	Postgraduate Certificate in Education
QCA	Qualification Curriculum Authority
QTS	Qualified teacher status
SEN	Special educational needs
SENCO	Special educational needs co-ordinator
TDA	Teacher Development Agency
TTA	Teacher Training Agency
UCET	Universities Council for the Education of Teachers
UNESCO	United Nations Educational, Cultural and Scientific Organization
YST	Youth Sport Trust

Chapter 1

The context for inclusion

Introduction and purpose of the book

Teaching is often referred to as both an art and a science and consequently requires a combination of creativity and innovation, matched by theoretical reflection and refinement. This book aims to address this eclectic approach to teaching children with special educational needs (SEN) in the physical education (PE) curriculum. The book will discuss and debate what can be considered as the essential theoretical elements of teaching children with SEN in PE, whilst offering opportunities for reflection on how these can be delivered in practice. In addition the book encourages you to 'think out of the box', be open to change, have open minds, and have high expectations of children with SEN and what they can achieve in PE, school sport and lifelong learning and participation in physical activity.

Whilst there is no one correct way of teaching or set of skills, techniques or protocols to follow, the book does set out to establish what can be considered as core principles of good practice. In order for you to ensure children with SEN have positive and successful learning experiences in PE, you as an individual teacher need to combine these core principles with your own individual uniqueness and experiences to produce the right mix for successful learning.

It is the intention that this book will act as a stimulus for thought and reflection, whatever stage of personal and professional development you are at (i.e. whether you are a trainee teacher, recently qualified, experienced practitioner, or working in an advisory or leadership capacity). Furthermore, the book will be of relevance to academics and those with a general interest in the area of disability sport and can be used as an opportunity to reflect on and review your current knowledge, understanding and delivery practices.

The book is structured around themed chapters which combine academic theory, research, practical application, reflective tasks and further reading. It is envisaged that this diverse approach will meet the individual needs of readers, whatever stage of development they are at. As a result the book sets out to:

- draw upon current research evidence and apply this to the practice of including children with SEN in PE;
- examine the statutory responsibilities that are placed upon teachers in relation to including children with SEN;
- combine academic theory with opportunities for critical reflection;
- provide a comprehensive range of tasks, issues and points for further debate;
- equip you with the knowledge, skills and understanding to ensure that children with SEN in PE learn and develop effectively.

The rise of the political and statutory inclusion agenda

In October 1997 the new Labour Government launched their Green Paper on special needs education, which stated:

> We want to see more pupils with special educational needs (SEN) included within mainstream primary and secondary schools. We support the United Nations Educational, Scientific and Cultural Organization (UNESCO) Salamanca World Statement on Special Needs Education 1994. This calls on governments to adopt the principle of inclusive education, enrolling all children in regular schools, unless there are compelling reasons for doing otherwise. This implies a progressive extension of the capacity of mainstream schools to provide for children with a wide range of needs.
>
> (DfEE 1997a: 44)

Since the return of the Labour Government to power in 1997, inclusion has risen up the political and statutory agenda in the United Kingdom (UK) to such an extent that there is widespread evidence of policies embedded across diverse sectors of society. In education, for example, there has been an increased emphasis on the inclusion of children with SEN through legislation such as the National Curriculum (NC) (2000) Inclusion Statement (QCA 1999c), SEN and Disability Rights Act (DfES 2001c) and the revised *Code of Practice* (DfES 2001b). In addition, the recent introduction of the Human Rights Act (Her Majesty's Stationery Office, 1998) and the Government's *Every Child Matters* (DfES 2004a) agenda have focused attention even more on the rights and responsibilities relating to children with SEN.

This UK-based picture mirrors similar developments in the USA associated with concepts of 'zero reject' and 'entitlement for all'. For example, the 'Public Law 94–142 Education for All Handicapped Children Act (1975)' in the USA set out to ensure children were given a fundamental right to access education, and have a clear statement of their SEN, which was subject to regular review. The law also enforced a requirement for states and localities to assess and ensure the effectiveness of their efforts to educate 'handicapped' children. Consequently, those responsible for the education of these children became accountable for the implementation of an appropriate education, within a context that was mindful of pupils' individual needs. Furthermore, many European countries have established similar statutory expectations on the inclusion of children with SEN which affirms the social drive for children to gain their entitlement and accessibility to an education which meets their individual needs.

In the UK, statistical evidence from the DfES (2004b) supports this increased emphasis on inclusion, and shows year on year rises in the number of children with SEN (i.e. registered on the Code of Practice) being included within mainstream education (2004 – 76 per cent, 2001 – 61 per cent, 1997 – 57 per cent, 1993 – 48 per cent). In addition, there is even greater pressure for teacher training providers, schools and teachers to reflect upon these issues because, as the NC (2000) states, 'teachers must take action' and 'ensure that their pupils are enabled to participate' (QCA 1999b: 33), and be responsive to a diverse range of pupil needs in order to facilitate inclusive education.

According to Avramadis and Norwich (2002), teachers are recognised as the main agents of the implementation of inclusive policy, and as such, 'without a coherent plan for teacher training in the educational needs of children with SEN, attempts to include these children in the mainstream would be difficult' (Avramadis and Norwich 2002: 139).

Depauw and Doll-Tepper (2000) support this view, and call for agencies such as Initial Teacher Training (ITT) providers, schools and teachers to review existing practices and procedures in order to provide a systematic approach to this area of their work. However, they question whether real change will actually occur, or if agencies and teachers are merely getting on the inclusion policy bandwagon, rather than fundamentally reviewing any necessary adjustment in working practices. Thus, they argue that in order for change to have impact you will need to recognise inclusion as a process model in which associated issues are infused throughout all of your teaching, learning, policy and practice aspects of your work. Therefore in order to produce positive PE experiences for children with SEN it is vital not merely to address issues at a superficial level, but more essentially to make a difference through inclusive delivery in practice. This book will help you to meet these expectations through a combination of theory, reflection and practical examples of including children with SEN in PE.

Setting high standards

In order to reflect the increasing emphasis on inclusion at government level, the recent NC review (culminating in NC 2000) set out four main priorities, one of which was to ensure that the curriculum is setting high standards for all pupils including the gifted, the talented and those with SEN. This supports the 1994 Salamanca Statement (UNESCO 1994), which identified a

Task 1.1 The Salamanca Statement

Reflect on the 1994 Salamanca Statement (UNESCO 1994), which establishes a set of beliefs and proclamations related to the notion that every child has a fundamental right to education. The statement identifies what are considered to be core principles of providing children with the **opportunity to learn, establishment of high standards, an education system designed to take account of diversity, access to regular child-centred education, and acceptance of inclusive orientation as a means of combating discrimination to build an inclusive society**. Using the table below, analyse what you understand by these terms, and how you can ensure they are delivered as part of your daily teaching and learning practice.

Key aspects of the Salamanca Statement (1994)	What do you understand the key aspect to be referring to, and how can you ensure this is delivered as part of your daily practice?
Providing children with an opportunity to learn	<ul><li>Understanding the individual needs of children;</li><li>matching my teaching to the needs of children;</li><li>being prepared to adapt and modify my teaching;</li><li>listening to the views of colleagues and working in partnership;</li><li>baseline assessments and ongoing review and evaluation of my teaching.</li></ul>
Establishing high standards and expectations of children with SEN	
Creating an education system designed to take account of diversity	
Access to regular child-centred education	
Acceptance of inclusion as a means of combating discrimination	

set of beliefs and proclamations relating to the notion that every child has a fundamental right to education. It identified core principles of providing children with the opportunity to learn, an education system designed to take account of diversity, access to regular child-centred education and the acceptance of inclusive orientation as a means of combating discrimination and building an inclusive society.

Therefore, through the introduction of recent inclusive legislation within the UK the notion of education for all, and entitlement, are viewed as central to the Government's drive to create a socially inclusive society in which all children are able to participate, learn and reach their full potential. This commitment is underpinned by the statement from the DfES that 'The education of children with special needs is a key challenge for the nation. It is vital to the creation of a fully inclusive society' (DfEE 1999: 1).

Delivering the inclusive agenda

In relation to teacher education, the Government's SEN *Excellence for All* (DfES 1998c) document suggests the educational achievements of pupils with SEN should be delivered through five key action points of:

- ensuring that high expectations are set for pupils with SEN;
- providing support to parents;
- increasing the numbers of pupils with SEN within mainstream education;
- emphasising the need for practical support, rather than procedural guidance;
- promoting partnerships in SEN at local, regional and national levels.

Therefore, with regard to how social inclusion is achieved, and the interpretation of its delivery within the curriculum, the Government introduced 'citizenship' as a curriculum area in its own right from September 2002. According to the NC handbooks for primary and secondary teachers (QCA 1999b, 1999c), citizenship will be delivered across all four key stages of the curriculum with the intention of facilitating pupils to 'become informed, active, responsible citizens contributing fully to the life of their school communities' (QCA 1999c: 126). Thus in doing so children will learn about 'their responsibilities, rights and duties as individuals and members of communities' (QCA 1999c: 126).

In interpreting this statement with reference to the inclusion of children with SEN, teachers are expected to establish a set of core values that can both be embedded within the statutory curriculum, and be delivered through proactive teaching and learning strategies. However, in order to facilitate these processes you need to be given opportunities to reflect and review the knowledge, understanding and practices that are necessary to implement these aspects of your professional delivery. PE does, however, offer many opportunities for children to learn mutual understanding and respect for each other which fulfils many aspects of the citizenship agenda within the NC.

However, the critical success factor that lies behind the successful inclusion of children with SEN within your PE lessons is the need to review the currency of your existing practices in order that the requirements of the NC (2000) Statutory Inclusion Statement (QCA 1999a) are met. These require you to address three key themes as part of your practice of including children with SEN in PE:

- set suitable learning challenges;
- respond to the diverse needs of pupils;
- differentiate your assessment and learning to meet the individual needs of pupils.

The first principle of the NC Inclusion Statement, 'setting suitable learning challenges', states, 'Teachers should aim to give every pupil the opportunity to experience success in learning and to achieve as high a standard as is possible' (QCA 1999a: 32). This will therefore require you to adopt flexible teaching and learning approaches and differentiate lessons according to pupil need. This links to the second aspect of the inclusion statement related to 'responding to pupils' diverse learning needs', in which it is stated that, 'When planning teachers should set high expectations and provide opportunities for all pupils to achieve including . . . pupils with disabilities and SEN' (QCA 1999a: 33).

Thus PE lessons should be planned to ensure full and effective access, and therefore you will be required to take specific action to respond to pupils' diverse learning needs. This can be achieved by creating effective learning environments; securing motivation and concentration; providing equality of opportunity through effective teaching approaches; and using relevant assessment strategies and targets for learning.

The third principle of the inclusion statement refers to 'overcoming potential barriers to learning and assessment for individuals and groups of pupils', and states, 'a minority of pupils will have particular learning and assessment requirements which go beyond the provisions described earlier (sections one and two)' (QCA 1999a: 35). However, if not addressed this could create barriers to participation and the NC states that this is usually as a consequence of a child's' disability or SEN. Thus, in suggesting methods to overcome potential barriers to participation, the curriculum suggests that in order to create access, greater differentiation on the part of teachers and the use of external agencies or specialist equipment will begin to enable inclusion to occur. Thus teachers need to be equipped with the necessary skills and expertise to facilitate this process.

Task 1.2 The National Curriculum Statutory Inclusion Statement
Look at three aspects of the National Curriculum (2000) Statutory Inclusion Statement and reflect upon how you can fulfil these requirements when including children with SEN in PE.

Aspect of the Statutory Inclusion Statement	Mechanisms to ensure it is delivered in practice
Setting suitable learning challenges	
Responding to pupils' diverse needs	
Differentiating assessment and learning to meet the individual needs of pupils	

In summary, the three guiding principles within the inclusion statement (which will be discussed further in chapter 4) are fundamental in ensuring that teachers recognise their responsibility of creating accessible lessons that cater for all pupils' needs.

The role of statutory and non-statutory agencies in supporting the inclusion agenda

The DfES acts as the government department 'established with the purpose of creating opportunity, releasing potential and achieving excellence for all' and 'delivers on a range of issues through working closely with other government departments and agencies' (DfES 2002: 1). Thus, through a range of legislative and policy-making strategies, they play a central role in setting the agenda for others in the delivery of education, PE and SEN.

In relation to the development, implementation, assessment and relevance of the NC, the Qualification Curriculum Authority (QCA) acts as 'a guardian of standards in education and training' and 'work[s] with others to maintain and develop the school curriculum and associated assessments and to accredit and monitor qualifications in schools' (QCA 2003: 1). They are responsible for ensuring that the PE NC meets the needs of all children and reflects the current and future generations' needs within society. Therefore they consult widely with others to ensure that the curriculum is relevant, broad, balanced and in keeping with the requirements of government and wider society.

In the backdrop of teacher training and the inspection of standards, the Teacher Development Agency (TDA) and Office for Standards in Education (OFSTED) play central roles in ensuring teachers are adequately prepared to include children with SEN. The TDA have responsibility for 'raising standards in schools' and 'improving the quality of teacher training and induction for newly qualified teachers' (TTA 2003b: 2).

In conjunction with this remit the TDA have established standards for the award of Qualified Teacher Status (QTS) and have national SEN specialist standards. The aim is to ensure that teachers are competently prepared through their ITT and future professional development training to maximise the learning and development that takes place with children with SEN in schools. In addition, through setting benchmark standards, they seek to ensure that teachers of the future have sufficient training and development opportunities to support children with SEN effectively once they are working in schools.

In contrast, the role of OFSTED is to: 'improve the quality of education . . . through independent inspection and regulation, and provide advice to the Secretary of State' (OFSTED 2003: 2).

Therefore, in the context of the training that takes place in ITT institutions, they are responsible for inspecting and reporting upon the quality and standards of delivery by these providers. Thus in relation to inclusion, the new Framework for Inspection (OFSTED 2002), requires OFSTED specifically to report on the delivery and implementation of aspects of equality of opportunity and inclusion, as well as disseminate any models of best practice that may be observed. Furthermore, as part of their inspection of schools, OFSTED focus aspects of their inspection on the extent to which teachers are meeting the statutory requirements of the Inclusion Statement in relation to children with SEN and the wider context of inclusion within school.

The professional PE associations and disability sport organisations

The professional PE associations and disability sport organisations are central to the successful implementation of the inclusion of children with SEN, from policy through to practice levels. Although the two PE associations – the British Association of Advisers and Lecturers in Physical Education (BAALPE) and the Physical Education Association (United Kingdom) (PEA (UK)) – do not have any statutory powers and responsibilities, their members play a vital role in ensuring that teachers are adequately prepared and supported to deliver the inclusive agenda within PE and school sport. They also play a key role in lobbying government and statutory agencies for effective change or guidance in order to ensure that current educational agendas are sufficiently met. In addition, they seek to produce resources and documentation that will assist their members to support children with SEN within mainstream PE. Refer to Further Reading (page 119) to find out more about the professional PE associations (who merge in late 2006 to become 'the Association for Physical Education').

In contrast, the English Federation for Disability Sport (EFDS) aims to: 'Serve as the main supporting and co-ordinating body for the development of sport for all disabled people' (English Federation for Disability Sport 1999: 36). In working towards this purpose EFDS has the direct support of all major disability sport organisations and aims to: increase the effectiveness of current disability sport structures; promote inclusion within mainstream programmes; access lottery funding; raise the profile of disability sport; and create networks and improve communication. Thus they have a central role to play in both lobbying and supporting PE and school sports agencies to deliver the Government's inclusion agenda and offer specialist advice, support and guidance to agencies and individuals.

In relation to the TDA standards for the award of QTS, the PE ITT providers are responsible for implementing the requirements as set out in the current 2002 framework. This framework, implemented in September 2002, supersedes the previous 10/97 (DfEE 1997c) and 4/98 (DfES 1998a) standards, and has a greater emphasis on issues of inclusion. Thus ITT providers and trainee teachers need to ensure that they are both meeting the requirements of the revised standards, and in turn be able to demonstrate that they are competently prepared to support children with SEN.

In relation to teacher training, ITT providers are recognised as playing a central role in ensuring that the PE teachers of the future are adequately prepared to deliver inclusive education. For example, in the Government's *SEN Excellence for All* document, one of the aims of the Government is to 'develop the knowledge and skills of staff working with children with SEN' and the programme plans to address this by 'giving greater emphasis to SEN within teacher training and development' (DfES 1998c: 7).

This was further emphasised in December 1999 through the TTA *National SEN Specialist Standards*, which stressed:

> The key to unlocking the full potential of pupils in our schools lies in the expertise of teachers and headteachers. Research and inspection evidence demonstrate the close correlation between the quality of teaching and the achievement of pupils.
>
> (TTA 1999: 1)

Thus the document recognised the central role that teachers and schools play, and for the first time began to identify aspects of SEN provision that are needed in order to create expertise and competence within this area of work. The document then goes on to further suggest:

> all teachers, whether in mainstream schools or in special schools, will need to continue to develop their teaching, pedagogy based on the known features of effective practice in meeting all pupils' learning needs.
>
> (TTA 1999: 3)

The key issue in the context of this chapter on setting the context for inclusion is the need for an examination of the role that government and statutory agencies have played in supporting PE teachers to deliver policy objectives that strongly advocate inclusion, as well as assisting them to gain the necessary professional standards for the award of QTS. The DfES SEN Programme of Action suggests, for example, that the Government 'is committed to ensuring that all teachers have the training and support they need to do their job well and are confident to deal with a wide variety of SEN' (DfES 1998b: 3). As a consequence, as policies and legislation change in relation to ITT and SEN, teachers, through their training, induction and continuing professional development, must be equipped with the necessary skills and support mechanisms to implement such policies effectively.

The DfES *Schools Achieving Success* (2001a) document suggests that the department will help schools to meet the needs of children with SEN through a commitment to inclusion and a recognition of the responsibility placed upon teachers to enable such practice to occur. According to Rose (1998), the central issue of concern is the extent to which ITT providers are helping teachers with the practical skills to deliver policy objectives that strongly advocate inclusion. Thus, the dual pressure of significant recognition of inclusion within the current 02/02 (TTA 2002) standards in tandem with increasing scrutiny of professional standards within ITT bring an acknowledgement that 'effective teaching depends on working well with everyone who has a stake in the education of our children' (TTA 2001a: 1).

Government legislation and regulation linked to SEN and teachers

Historically the UK Government has supported, and maintained through legislation and policies a significant infrastructure of segregated schools. However, there is a long-established tradition of encouraging mainstream schools to make some form of provision that was recognisably 'special', and guidance has been offered as to what this provision should consist of. It is not only in ITT that the government has set out policies, but over many years conventional expectations for the provision of schooling for children with SEN have been apparent.

Since the emergence of the first significant (in terms of SEN) piece of educational legislation with the 1944 Education Act (DoE 1944), it is only in more recent times through introduction of the NC (QCA 1999a) and the 02/02 (TTA 2002) standards for the award of QTS that some synergy of policy in education in schools, and education in ITT related to inclusion has begun to emerge. Thus, in order for the Government's inclusion agenda to become a reality in schools, there is a need to ensure that the policies and agendas of respective agencies work in tandem, to complement, rather than work against, each other. For example, as the NC (2000) increased its emphasis on SEN through the Statutory Inclusion Statement, this should also be reflected in an increased emphasis within ITT standards.

The 1944 Education Act (DoE 1944) was the first piece of legislation that established separate schooling for pupils of different aptitudes and abilities. These were established through separate forms of special education with different types of schools, for different forms of disability related to a total of eleven medically defined categories of handicap (Fredrickson and Cline 2002). However, the Act placed a duty on local education authorities (LEAs) of the time to ascertain the needs of children with SEN, and anticipated that treatment in many cases may be best served in mainstream education.

The reality for many teachers training to work in mainstream schools, however, was that the issue of disability, handicap, and the education of such children were rarely addressed. At the time this was seen as the role of special school teachers, who had the knowledge to work with such pupils, rather than educating them alongside their non-disabled peers, where mainstream teachers were ill equipped to support them. This situation remained largely unchanged until the publication of the Warnock Report in 1978 (DES 1978), which acknowledged that around 18 per cent of school pupils could be expected to have special needs, and reinforced that the majority of these needs should be met in the mainstream. This change in policy, culminating in the 1981 Education Act (DES 1981), in which 'statementing' (a formal process of identifying, assessing and supporting a child with SEN) was introduced, brought more mainstream teachers into contact with children with SEN. In conjunction with this requirement, there was no formal ITT stipulation for teachers to be trained to support this goal. Consequently, as more children with SEN integrated into mainstream schools, few if any teachers or training providers had spent time adequately considering the needs of these children. As a result, the changing policy directives reflected in schools were not being developed alongside changes in ITT provision, thus demonstrating a distinct lack of co-ordination and multi-agency working.

In 1994, the *Code of Practice on the Identification and Assessment of Special Educational Needs* (DES 1994) was introduced, which brought with it a designation of clear roles and responsibilities that schools must adopt in order to support children with SEN. This has since been replaced by the new *Code of Practice* (DfES 2001b), which takes account of the SEN and Disability Act (DfES 2001c) and puts a stronger emphasis on children with SEN being educated in the mainstream. In addition, rights of statutory assessment and duties of local education authorities to arrange services to support parents and help resolve any matters of conflict were further emphasised. Thus, with the increasing emphasis of inclusion being placed upon schools, the need to ensure teachers were given the appropriate training in ITT is self-evident, and this began to be reflected (although only minimally) in the 4/98 (DfES 1998a) standards for the award of QTS.

In support of this position, the Universities Council for the Education of Teachers (UCET) response to the Government's SEN Green Paper in 1997 stated that:

> There is some evidence from research and OFSTED reports that pupils benefit where teachers are trained in SEN. We recommend that there is a need for research into their training needs for successful inclusion.
>
> (UCET 1997b: 2)

In addition, Ainscow *et al.* suggest:

> The government green paper *Excellence for All Children: Meeting SEN* places the issue of inclusion at the centre of discussions on the development of policy and practice for pupils with special needs.
>
> (Ainscow *et al.* 1999: 9)

Task 1.3 Developing a cohesive framework for inclusive PE
Reflect upon what you would see as the positive features of establishing a cohesive framework to support PE teachers to deliver inclusion for children with SEN. As part of your analysis you should look at what you understand by the different roles each agency (i.e. DfES, OFSTED, TDA, ITT providers and professional PE and disability associations) play in ensuring pupils with SEN receive positive experiences in PE.

Agency	What role do you see the agencies playing in order to provide a cohesive framework for inclusive PE?
Department for Education and Skills (DfES)	
Office for Standards in Education (OFSTED)	
Teacher Development Agency (TDA)	
ITT providers	
Professional PE Associations (Association for PE)	
English Federation for Disability Sport (EFDS)	

Thus, the need for government educational policy within schools to match the ITT policy can be seen as a critical success factor in ensuring that the needs of children with SEN in mainstream schools are adequately met. This further strengthened the need for agencies such as DfES, OFSTED, TDA and ITT providers to work together within a cohesive framework to support PE teachers to deliver inclusion for children with SEN.

Implementing teacher training and SEN policy in practice: a multi-agency approach to a multi-agency challenge for PE teachers?

The DfES *Schools Achieving Success* states, 'We will not rest until we have a truly world class education system that meets the needs of every child. Whatever it takes' (DfES 2001a: 7). The Government seeks to realise this desire by aiming to 'develop multi-agency working. Too often different support agencies do not work effectively together' (DfES 2001a: 22).

The Government, DfES and agencies like the TDA and OFSTED, play a critical role in ensuring that partnership, collaboration and joined-up thinking are fostered in order to ensure that future generations of PE teachers are equipped to deliver the Government's objective of a truly world-class education system, which includes meeting fully the needs of children with SEN. Specifically in relation to children with SEN in school contexts, the DfES have stated that: 'a framework will be developed to measure the effectiveness of school and LEA programmes for raising standards for children with special needs' (DfES 2001a: 22). The DfES will seek to implement this through the development of benchmark standards and performance tools to compare attainment, so mainstream and special schools can evaluate how they are doing in relation to other schools. However, whilst this brings with it further regulation and monitoring of schools, it does give all stakeholders the opportunity to measure the extent to which progress is being made to support children with SEN.

The Government suggests that in regard to the formal assessment of benchmark standards, 'OFSTED inspection will look at schools' development of inclusive practice' (DfES 2001a: 22). In relation to school inspection, OFSTED believes:

> An educationally inclusive school is one in which the teaching and learning, achievements, attitudes and well being of every young person matter. Effective schools are educationally inclusive schools. This shows not only in their performance, but also in their ethos and their willingness to offer new opportunities to pupils who have experienced difficulties.
> (OFSTED 2002: 4)

Therefore, in relation to school contexts, OFSTED will consider whether all pupils get a fair deal, how well schools recognise and overcome barriers to learning, and whether the school's values embrace inclusion and promote it openly and proactively. In addition, they will look at the extent to which teachers have taken account of the three principles of the NC Inclusion Statement, and consider, from an ITT perspective, whether trainees and training providers are meeting the QTS standards to ensure inclusive schooling for children with SEN.

Supporting teachers to effectively include children with SEN

In looking to support teachers both during training and once working in schools, various agencies responsible for teacher training have over time published documents to ensure that trainees are sufficiently equipped and prepared to meet the demands of the teaching profession. For example, the development and revision of standards for the awards of QTS have emerged out of several government circulars (3/84, 24/89, 9/92, 14/93, 10/97, 4/98 (DfES 1998a)) and have culminated in the current 02/02 'Professional Standards Framework' (TTA 2002). The intention and rationale for further prescription of standards for teacher training in part came out of a desire by the TDA to look at a full codification of training expectations and monitor these through OFSTED. The first significant recognition of the need to ensure teachers have a full appreciation of SEN and inclusion came through the DfES (1998) *SEN Excellence for All* publication. This stated that government planned to give 'greater emphasis to SEN within teacher training and development' (DfES 1998c: 6).

This culminated in the development of the TTA *National SEN Specialist Standards* (TTA 1999), which were designed as an audit tool to help teachers and head teachers identify specific training and development needs related to the effective teaching of SEN. The TTA state within the *National SEN Specialist Standards*:

> As the government's intention to increase opportunities for pupils with severe and/or complex SEN to be educated within mainstream school is realised, teachers will need a basic understanding of the range of SEN to be found in most mainstream classes, and more teachers in mainstream schools require the knowledge, understanding and skills to work effectively with pupils with severe and or complex SEN.
>
> (TTA 1999: 3, point 9)

In support of this view, the *SEN Excellence for All* (DfES 1998) fourth action point is of particular relevance to teacher training in that the document specifically states its intentions to 'develop the knowledge and skills of staff working with children with SEN' (DfES 1998c: 4).

As a result, in order to ensure all teachers have the training and support needed to do their job well, and are confident in dealing with a wide range of SEN, a clearer strategy position was starting to be formulated. Since this time further publications have arisen such as the Centre for Studies in Inclusive Education (2000) *Index for Inclusion*, which provides schools with a framework to audit existing practices and plan for the development of fully inclusive cultures within schools.

The teacher training process from day one, through ITT, award of QTS, induction and lifelong continuing professional development

The TDA acknowledges the teaching profession is based upon 'reflective practice', and a recognition that teachers' knowledge and understanding develop and grow over a lifetime of work with children. As a consequence, in relation to teachers of PE, it is important to recognise that training in inclusive education for children with SEN must involve several agencies working together in partnership to ensure that learning and development processes work effectively.

The TTA *National SEN Specialist Standards* (TTA 1999) advocate that the 4/98 (DfES 1998a) (and now subsequent 02/02 (TTA 2002)) standards will be the main vehicle for measuring competence within ITT. They argue that as more children with SEN enter mainstream, 'more teachers in mainstream schools will require the knowledge, understanding and skills to work effectively with pupils' (TTA 1999: 3, point 9). It goes on to suggest that 'all teachers, whether in mainstream schools or in special schools, will need to continue to develop their teaching pedagogy based on the known features of effective practice in meeting all pupils' learning needs' (TTA 1999: 3, point 10). In relation to outcomes of the training process, Cheminas notes that under the new *Code of Practice* for SEN (DfES 2001b) implemented in 2002 comes an expectation that OFSTED will have a responsibility to inspect and report upon 'the impact of the school's strategies for promoting inclusion' (Cheminas 2000: 52).

In addition, Cheminas (2000) notes that in evaluating inclusion within schools, OFSTED will be ensuring that the training teachers receive in ITT is effective once they come to teach in schools.

Through the 4/98 (DfES 1998a), and now 02/02 (TTA 2002) standards, the DfES, TTA and OFSTED have firmly supported the policy that, by establishing standards for newly qualified teachers (NQTs), this will help raise competence. However, questions still remain as to the extent of student trainees' knowledge relating to SEN, and the appropriateness of the standards that have been identified as essential prerequisites prior to qualifying. Therefore, whilst standards give the general area to be developed, it is a matter of professional judgement by the ITT provider and schools as to how this is achieved, and the extent to which competence has been attained. In addition, there is much debate around the use of terms such as 'competence' and how this can be clearly demonstrated, interpreted and evidenced within ITT programmes (Dyson 2001).

Conclusion

The 02/02 'Professional Standards Framework' for the award of QTS developed by the TDA (TTA 2002) go some way towards ensuring teachers have high expectations of all pupils including those with SEN; promote positive values; understand their responsibilities under the *Code of Practice*; differentiate teaching; respond to a diverse range of learning needs; and recognise and respond to equal opportunity issues. As noted at the start of this chapter, the inclusion of children with SEN and the development of quality learning experiences in PE has risen up both the statutory and political agenda. There is now a whole raft of policy expectations that are placed on trainee teachers, experienced practitioners and those with a vested interest in the education of children with SEN. Teaching is a profession that requires you to reflect upon your knowledge, understanding and personal commitment to maximise opportunities for children with SEN to be engaged in positive PE experiences. The following chapters will begin to address some of the key aspects of your training and continuing professional development that aim to prepare you for ensuring children with SEN have teachers with high expectations of them, whilst matching the curriculum to their specific needs. As a consequence, in addition to fulfilling the statutory expectations placed upon trainee and qualified PE teachers, a readiness to be flexible, open to change and responsive to the needs of individual pupils with SEN can be seen as central to successful learning experiences.

Chapter 2

Children with special educational needs

Introduction

This chapter maps the history of SEN from the position of segregation and isolation, through to the emergence, development and future directions of the inclusion movement of today. It examines how legislation and policy directions have transformed special education, and the impact upon children, teachers and schools. The evolution of terminology and language will also be analysed, with particular reference to its principles and implementation in practice.

The chapter does not set out to provide extensive, detailed lists of what each SEN comprises and how you should support children with their specific needs. Rather, it seeks to outline general principles and strategies for identifying and supporting children with SEN within a context of consultation and empowerment. Consequently, in relation to identifying the needs of children with SEN, if it simply came down to the provision of robotic protocols of how to support people, first it would miss the complexity of human nature, and second it would not take any account of the interrelationship of individuality, personality, uniqueness of the teacher and the child, and the environment within which you are working. Thus the chapter seeks to identify some fundamental principles which will help you support children's learning and development in PE, whilst gaining an insight into the specific needs and support they may require.

The development of special needs education has over time produced a complex picture within which several competing theories have contributed to the modern day 'inclusive' stance. Norwich, for example, argues that 'There is no logical purity in education' (Norwich 2002a: 483), rather there is 'ideological impurity', in which no single value or principle encompasses all of what is considered worthwhile. As a result, there needs to be recognition of a range of 'multiple values' (Norwich 2002a: 483) through which a series of interrelated concepts and ideologies are acknowledged as contributing to contemporary views on inclusion for children with SEN.

This rather convoluted analysis of developments, definitions and interpretations of inclusion is further acknowledged by authors such as Ainscow *et al.* 1999, Ballard 1997, Barton 1997, Croll and Moses 2000, Dyson 1999, Dyson and Millward 2000, and Fredrickson and Cline 2002. Therefore, in the context of Norwich's view of logical impurity this reaffirms the intention of this chapter to identify general principles and strategies to support children with SEN rather than seek to produce detailed protocols of specific needs which oversimplifies the complexity of your teaching and learning strategies and the individuality of children.

The context and emergence of inclusion

Dyson and Millward (2000) suggest the Government Green Paper on SEN (DfEE 1997a) was the first time that the UK Government had avowedly committed itself to creating an inclusive education system. This was significant in that it indicated a commitment by the Government to two central themes.

First, it 'signalled an intention to shake special needs provision out of the somewhat complacent state in which, it is arguable, it had rested for the past two decades' (Dyson and Millward 2000: 1). For example, since the introduction of the Warnock Report in 1978 (DES 1978), culminating in the 1981 Education Act (DES 1981), the notion of children with SEN moving from special into mainstream schools was largely taken for granted. Progress during the period from 1978 to 1997 was in Dyson and Millward's (2000) view *ad hoc*, in that it supported integration, but gave no firm steer to how LEAs should implement this. This is broadly in line with policy developments in ITT in which, prior to the 4/98 (DfES 1998a) and 02/02 Professional Standards Framework (TTA 2002), guidance was given through a series of Government circulars (i.e. 3/84, 24/89, 9/92, 10/97), but with no firm instructions in relation to SEN. Consequently, some local education authorities moved further than others and, as a result, since the introduction of the 1981 Education Act there had been no significant shift towards a more integrated system (Swann 1985, 1988, 1992).

Second, the 1997 Green Paper brought alignment with the Salamanca Statement (UNESCO 1994), formulated in an agreement between 94 governments, and 25 international organisations. This, according to authors such as Pijl *et al.* (1997), recognised the extent to which inclusion had now become a 'global agenda', as well as advocating genuine recognition and commitment to the term 'inclusion'. The Salamanca Statement argued:

> The challenge confronting the inclusive school is that of developing a child-centred pedagogy capable of successfully educating all children, including those who have serious disadvantages and disabilities. The merit of such schools is not only that they are capable of providing quality education for all children; their establishment is a crucial step in helping

to change discriminatory attitudes, in creating welcoming communities and in developing an inclusive society.

(UNESCO 1994: 6–7)

The emergence of this contemporary position is a far cry from the mid 1800s, when the first special schools were established (Fredrickson and Cline 2002). These were intended to provide for children with severe hearing or visual difficulty who could not learn in ordinary schools alongside existing school provision, and places were offered only to upper and middle class pupils. In the late nineteenth century, as more children were educated from diverse backgrounds, schools were not accustomed to such diversity of learning needs. Increasing numbers of children were therefore excluded, as payment to schools at the time was 'by results'.

This rejection of children who were entitled to an education under the 1870 Education Act (DoE 1870) led to an expansion in special school provision (Fredrickson and Cline 2002). Thus, children who were perceived as 'handicapped' were seen as different from other children, and educated in separate schools. This separate provision remained largely static up until the mid 1960s when authors such as Dunn (1968) acknowledged there was a lack of evidence that disabled children educated in special schools did any better than those who were being educated in mainstream schools. Consequently arguments for 'reverse separation' (Fedrickson and Cline 2002) began to emerge, prompting a move towards more integrated school structures within the UK.

Task 2.1 Advantages and disadvantages of inclusive PE

Using the table below identify what you see as the advantages and potential disadvantages of including children with SEN in mainstream PE lessons. You should consider this from three perspectives: you as the teacher, the child with SEN and non-disabled pupils.

	Advantages	Potential disadvantages
Inclusive PE (disabled and non-disabled pupils educated alongside each other)		
Segregated PE (disabled and non-disabled pupils taught in separate lessons)		

Development of a continuum of needs

In 1970 the Education (Handicapped Children) Act (DoE 1970) removed the legal distinction between those who were, and were not educable within schools. According to Mittler (1985), this rapidly transformed the educational experience of children with SEN, including those with severe learning difficulties, and saw a growth in the skills of teachers and a development of the curriculum, in what Coupe (1986) described as the 'new special schools'. A key feature of this shift in provision was that the education of children with disabilities moved from the responsibility of government departments of health to that of education. This follows similar developments in the USA associated with concepts of 'zero reject' and 'entitlement for all'.

The principle of 'normalisation', focusing on commonalities between children rather than differences, also began to emerge with ideas that:

> the aims of education for children and young people with disabilities and other children are the same as those for all children and young people . . . Disabilities and significant difficulties do not diminish the right to and equal access to participation in society.
>
> (Inner London Education Authority 1985)

In the UK, similar developments in the Education Act 1981 (DES 1981) introduced the legally defined term SEN, following advice from the 1978 Warnock Report (DES 1978). Prior to this time, provision focused upon identifying schooling for the 'handicapped'. The Warnock Report recommended statutory categories of handicap (other than maladjustment) be abolished, and children with SEN to be identified by individual and detailed profiles of their needs following assessment. Warnock indicated that it was not appropriate to focus attention merely on a small proportion of children with severe difficulties, which gave a sharp distinction between the disabled and non-disabled. Thus, a child should not be assigned to a particular category, but rather SEN should be acknowledged on a continuum with ordinary needs. Consequently the recommendation was made that school provision should not be either 'segregated' or 'mainstream', but on a dimension, which took account of children's individual needs.

The Education Act 1981 (DES 1981) (introduced to implement the recommendations of the 1978 Warnock Report) brought a shift towards assessment of SEN, rather than the diagnosis of disability which had been previously used to categorise, and isolate, children. This supported similar developments at the time associated with the development of 'medical and social models' of disability (Reiser and Mason 1990). Social models of disability acknowledge that once a child's individual learning needs are established through assessment, schools and teachers must respond accordingly and plan to meet their particular learning requirements. In contrast, 'medical models' of disability view the learning difficulty as located with the child and, as such, once assessed they would be placed into existing, unchanged provision, or placed in segregated school structures.

Focuses of causation

The location and cause of SEN has been subject to much debate (Fredrickson and Cline 2002, Reiser and Mason 1990, Farrell 2001, Lloyd 2000), and various approaches have been suggested which consider what or whom the disabling factor in a child's education is. In support of developments in medical and social models of disability, Fredrickson and Cline (2002) indicate that a combination of individual differences, environmental demands and interactional analyses have contributed to differing perspectives on the inclusion of children with SEN.

They propose that **models of individual difference** (medical models) are embodied in legislation prior to introduction of the Education Act 1981 (DES 1981), and are particularly emphasised in the Education Act 1944 (DoE 1944), which was dominated by disability of body or mind. Consequently, individual differences were considered along a range of biological, behavioural or cognitive domains, with causation located firmly with the child, and no acknowledgement of contributory factors external to the child, such as quality of teaching. This rather dated view is distinct from what was acknowledged in the *Code of Practice on the Identification and Assessment of Special Educational Needs* (DES 1994), which advocated that 'schools should not automatically assume that children's learning difficulties always result solely or even mainly from problems within the child. The school's practices can make a difference – for good or ill' (DES 1994: para. 2.19).

Therefore, the quality of teaching and learning delivered by the teacher, the ability to be equipped with the necessary skills to support children with SEN, and school cultures are significant factors in making inclusion a success or failure (Centre for Studies in Inclusive Education 2000).

In contrast to medical and individual models of disability, **environmental models** emerged which adopted a situation-focused, rather than a person-centred focus, to inclusive provision. This suggests that SEN can only be defined in terms of relationships between what a person can do, and what a person must do to succeed in any given environment. Fredrickson and Cline suggest that 'at one extreme then, the environmentally focused approach holds that there are no children with learning difficulties, only adults with teaching difficulties' (Fredrickson and Cline 2002: 40).

This supports the work of Seamus Hegarty who in the 1980s advocated that children should be placed on a 'continuum of provision', that should equate to discrete categories of need. As a consequence, rather than attempting to adapt the child to the environment and see the disability as located with the child (medical model), schools and teachers conversely should be looking to how they can modify their learning environments (social model) in order that it meets the individual needs of children. As a result this necessitates schools and teachers to be prepared to think in different ways and recognise that there are many methods and strategies that can be utilised to support the inclusion of children with SEN (Ainscow *et al.* 1999, Skrtic 1995, Dyson and Millward 2000).

Interactional models advocate impossibility in separating the learning competencies of individual children from the environment within which they live and function (Booth 1993, Keogh *et al.* 1997). Models of disability, causation and location are seen as a combination of complex interactions between the strengths and weaknesses of the child, levels of support available and the appropriateness of education being provided. Thus, neither environmental nor individual approaches on their own fit the particular reality of SEN in schools, and 'special educational needs are often not just a reflection of pupils' inherent difficulties or disabilities; they are often related to factors within schools which can prevent or exacerbate problems' (National Curriculum Council 1989: para. 5).

This view has been further endorsed in the *Code of Practice*, which suggests, 'It should be recognised that some difficulties in learning may be caused or exacerbated by the school's learning environment or adult/child relationships' (DfES 2001b: para 5.6).

Task 2.2 Focuses of causation

Using the table below review your understanding of the three proposed focuses of causation of disability, namely individual differences (medical models), environmental demands (social models) and interaction analyses. You should consider these in relation to developing your understanding of the terms and implications for your practice.

	Interpretation of what each focus of causation stands for	Implications for your practice
Individual differences (medical models)		
Environmental demands (social models)		
Interactional analyses (combination of the two)		

In addition, the revised *Code of Practice* (DfES 2001b) asks for schools to look within existing provision (School Action and School Action Plus), rather than regularly seek external advice and support as a means of addressing individual children's needs.

Therefore, in order to respond to the needs of children with SEN at a more localised level, teachers need as part of their professional development to be given opportunities to examine the impact of school cultures and pedagogical practices on either enabling or restricting inclusive education. This in part is now being addressed through the 02/02 'Professional Standards Framework' (TTA 2002) in which trainee teachers are required to have high expectations of all pupils, promote positive values, differentiate, and respond to individual needs, and understand their responsibilities under the Code of Practice. As a result teachers are now required to think in many different ways about how their teaching approaches can enhance or deny access to an inclusive education for children with SEN.

Contradictions in attempts to plan for inclusive practice

In deducing how education systems in schools respond to diversity, Artiles (1998) suggests there is a 'dilemma of difference' within which fundamental mass education systems are established to deliver all students an 'education'. Mass education has, for instance, basic features of a common core of skills and knowledge, delivered in broadly equivalent circumstances, in schools with similar levels of training and pedagogies which do not vary significantly from school to school.

However, if education is to fulfil the diversity it demands, Artiles (1998) suggests this can only be achieved by acting at individual pupil levels, which recognise children are different from each other. Pertinent to this is the need to construct and engage learning strategies that recognise different interests, aptitudes and expectations. This dilemma and tension brings with it difficulties in planning an appropriate education for children with special needs. As a consequence, there is:

> a dilemma in education over how difference is taken into account – whether to recognise differences as relevant to individual needs by offering different provision, but in doing so could reinforce unjustified inequalities, and is associated with devaluation; or, whether to offer a common and valued provision for all but with the risk of not providing what is relevant to individual needs.
>
> (Norwich 1994: 293)

This picture recognises the development of educational policy in SEN over many years. The 1944 Education Act (DoE 1944) formalised a common education structure, in which all children were placed into different forms of schooling. The 1970s then involved increasing exploration of how far all children could be included within the same school, and in the 1980s the NC emerged, along with an exploration of mixed ability classes and concepts of differentiation. In the late 1990s and early part of the twenty-first century, and as a consequence of this evolving provision, Dyson and Millward suggest 'it is more helpful to think of inclusion as an outcome of actions within a school rather than as an inherent characteristic of the school' (Dyson and Millward 2000: 170).

Thus the measure of the extent to which inclusion is demonstrated in practice comes through the observation and charting of 'real life' case studies of children engaged in inclusive schools (Ainscow 1999). As a result, teachers of the future need to be equipped with the knowledge, understanding and strategies to enable inclusion to become a reality, and to be enabled to demonstrate this in outcomes that indicate positive experiences for children with SEN. As a consequence, according to Westwood (1997), the place to develop this teaching philosophy is as part of a trainee teacher's ITT.

Dilemmatic resolutions

Inclusive, and SEN, provision has been subject to 'a succession of dilemmatic resolutions' (Dyson and Millward 2000: 173) which have changed and emerged over many years. In addition, factors such as the introduction of the NC, OFSTED inspection and development of the *Code of Practice* (DfES 2001b) have signalled an ever-increasing scrutiny and control by Government on many issues of provision within schools. This brings with it a pressure between the espoused policy of schools, and policies pursued nationally by government and statutory agencies (Dyson 2001, Lloyd 2000). Consequently, joined-up and collaborative approaches to inclusive education are essential if they are to become a reality for children with SEN. To some extent, in agencies such as OFSTED with dual roles of inspection of ITT and school-based provision, this does give a better appreciation of what the issues and needs of the future are. Thus, more of this type of dual, or joint agency working is to be further encouraged through the DfES *Schools Achieving Success* (DfES 2001a) publication, in which an increased emphasis is placed on collaboration.

In the post-war years the education of children was largely by groupings of ability, in which 'streaming' was very much the order of the day as a means of integrating all pupils into mainstream contexts. Tansley and Guildford (1960) argue this was with the intention of not segregating people, but providing specialist provision through what at the time were referred to as 'remedial classes'. However, authors such as Carroll 1972, Collins 1972, and Galloway and Goodwin 1979, criticised this provision for its segregatory and stigmatising nature, and consequently streaming was seen as limiting the life opportunities to which children with special needs had access. This led to experiments with remedial work, and a shift in attention to 'whole class approaches' to teaching all pupils. This movement in thinking resulted in an emergence of 'whole school approaches' (Clark *et al.* 1995b), through which teachers would look to accommodate needs within the classroom, rather than through separate (remedial) classrooms and special needs teachers. This necessitated a change in curriculum pedagogy, in which ordinary classes became fully accessible, with additional teacher support, and the role of the remedial teacher began to develop into one of a special educational needs co-ordinator (SENCO). As a result, teachers of the future need to be given the necessary support and training within their ITT, and continuing professional development to reflect upon the impact that their pedagogical practices can have in contributing to either positive or negative learning experiences. In addition, as part of their training teachers need to know how to work collaboratively in order to provide a holistic approach to a child with SEN involving parents, support workers, health care professionals and the like.

Liberal principles and interchangeable terminology

In moving towards a more integrated structure of SEN provision, Clark *et al.* (1995b) suggest educational developments have been driven through relatively liberal principles. Whilst these principles have been contested, the history and development of special needs education in the UK are in tune with what we now term 'inclusion' (Dyson 1999). Consequently, the education system has been influenced through moderate principles of equity, valuing pupils' individual rights to participate, curricula learning experiences and recognition that 'the purpose of education for all children is the same, the goals are the same' (Warnock Report, DES 1978: 1.4).

The key challenge for educationalists, though, is how this is interpreted in practice and provision for children with SEN within inclusive environments. Additionally, in relation to ITT providers, the challenge is to be able to equip teachers of the future with the necessary skills to respond to the requirements of the inclusion movement.

Lloyd (2000) suggests:

> rather than developing inclusive approaches to practice in mainstream education, the integration of pupils with SEN has served to perpetuate and reinforce segregated practices, placing the impetus for change on the pupil.

(Lloyd 2000: 135)

Many factors have contributed to this viewpoint, which have mainly arisen out of 'fundamental misunderstanding and confusion about the concepts of integration and inclusion, and indeed the term SEN itself' (Lloyd 2002: 111). Dyson (2001), for example, argues there is a lack of consensus on what constitutes an equal education, failure to recognise all children's rights to learn, lack of how to identify SEN and the resistance of practitioners to change. As a consequence, there is a need for significant debate and common ground to be established on what the related terms mean in policy and practice (Lloyd 2000, Farrell 1998, Dyson 2001, Dyson and Millward 2000). If this first stage of clarification is not achieved, then the various stakeholders involved in the inclusion of children with SEN are going to be potentially working against rather than with each other to promote inclusive educations (Depauw and Doll-Tepper 2000).

Within the UK, 'SEN' was introduced as a legally defined term in the Education Act 1981 (DES 1981) and 'refers to children's learning needs in school . . . is legally defined and this legal definition is used to decide whether particular children are eligible for special educational services' (Fredrickson and Cline 2002: 34).

In contrast, 'special needs' is not legally defined, and refers to needs experienced by pupils from most of the school population (i.e. homeless children, English as an additional language (EAL) pupils and those from unstable family environments). As a consequence, the terms 'SEN' and 'special needs' are often used interchangeably (Dyson 2001, Ainscow et al. 1999) and this can 'cause unhelpful confusion since individuals from groups who have special needs may or may not have SEN' (Fredrickson and Cline 2002: 34).

In relation to 'integration', Ainscow (1995) suggests this is concerned with making a limited number of additional arrangements for individual pupils with SEN in schools, which as an outcome result in little change overall. In contrast, inclusion is concerned with the introduction of more radical changes through which schools restructure themselves in order to embrace all children. Thus integration involves a process of assimilating an individual into existing structures, whilst inclusion is more concerned with accommodation, where the onus is on the school to change (Dyson 2001, Dyson and Millward 2000). However, despite the conceptual distinction between the two terms they are often (like special needs and SEN) used as synonyms for each other (Thomas et al. 1998).

Consequently, this is an issue in need of further clarification at all levels from government policy through to professional practice with teachers. For example, at the policy level there is a need to be clear about what the terms mean in order to set clear expectations and resource inclusion effectively. At the professional opinion and practice (ITT provider) level trainee teachers need to be equipped with a full appreciation of the history, context and interpretation of terminology. If this is successfully achieved through delivery in schools by PE teachers there is a greater likelihood of inclusion becoming a reality for children with SEN.

Interpretations of inclusion

Concepts of inclusion have been subject to extensive debate in terms of their meaning and interpretation related to SEN. Ballard, a New Zealand scholar, notes, for example:

> Inclusive education means education that is non-discriminatory in terms of disability, culture, gender or other aspects of students or staff that are assigned significance by a society. It involves all students in a community, with no exceptions and irrespective of their intellectual, physical, sensory or other differences, having equal rights to access the culturally valued curriculum of their society as full-time valued members of age-appropriate mainstream classes. Inclusion emphasises diversity over assimilation, striving to avoid the colonisation of minority experiences by dominant modes of thought and action.
>
> (Ballard 1997: 244–245)

According to authors such as Booth (1995) and Dyson and Millward (2000), this definition is highly content specific and refers more to aspects of cultural diversity, rather than special needs education. They argue that the 1994 Salamanca Statement's interpretation of inclusion refers predominantly to finding basic forms of education for marginalised street children, working children, and those living in remote areas. In contrast, Dyson and Millward (2000) suggest inclusion within the UK has stronger links to its emergence through the work of Skrtic (1991, 1995) and Fuchs and Fuchs (1994), in which the American notion of inclusion grew out of a different social policy history based on civil rights, with particular reference to race, and more recently the philosophy has been transferred to the education of children with SEN.

Booth *et al.* suggest:

> Inclusion is a set of never ending processes. It involves the specification of the direction of change. It is relevant to any school however inclusive or exclusive its current cultures, policies and practices. It requires schools to engage in a critical examination of what can be done to increase the learning and participation of the diversity of students within the school locality.
>
> (Booth *et al.* 2000: 12)

As a consequence, Daniels and Garner (1999) argue that, whilst it is important to recognise that inclusion can have global agreement (Pijl *et al.* 1997), it is vital that inclusion is specifically interpreted within each national system. The development of inclusion and SEN within the UK should be considered therefore in terms of its particular history, culture and politics of its specific emerging system. As a consequence, it is 'dangerous to see the recent adoption of the inclusion agenda by the UK Government as a straightforward alignment with a policy direction that is both globally understood and relatively straightforward' (Dyson and Millward 2000: 4). As a result, the relationship between inclusion and SEN needs to be specifically aligned to the UK education system and Government provision in order to fully appreciate its underlying philosophies and practices.

Task 2.3 Terminology

Review your understanding of the distinctions between the terms SEN, special needs, integration and inclusion. How do you think having a clearer understanding and appreciation of these terms will help you in your practice of ensuring children with SEN gain positive PE experiences?

Changing school approaches: the shift from integration to inclusion

The difference between integration and inclusion is that the former applies to ways of supporting students with special needs in essentially unchanged mainstream schools. However, the latter refers to a radical restructuring of schools in order that they are inherently capable of educating all students within their communities (Corbett and Slee 2000, Sebba and Sachdev 1997). However, Dyson and Millward (2000) argue that this interpretation is too simplistic to apply to the UK system, in a background of longstanding expectations of mainstream schools to educate children with SEN. As a result, these expectations have involved the exploration of 'whole school approaches', in which teachers were required to consider 'fundamental changes in practice and organisation' (Dyson and Millward 2000: 8). This exploration has led to the dissolving of boundaries between special and mainstream education, as well as categories of special and ordinary children: 'and whole school response will essentially be a response to meeting the individual needs of children' (Dessent 1987: 121).

In examining the concept of 'whole school approaches', the emergence of the NC (2000) (QCA 1999a) has added impetus to this shift, with its emphasis through the Statutory Inclusion Statement on setting suitable learning challenges, responding to individual diversity and differentiating assessment. Consequently, in the years following the introduction of the NC, a number of schools were 'moving "beyond the whole school approach" in this sense towards what we chose to call "innovatory practice" in schools' approaches to special needs' (Dyson and Millward 2000: 10).

Thus according to Dyson and Millward (2000) school provision centred upon conceptualising approaches in terms of responses to student diversity as a whole, rather than simply a response to special needs; merging of special needs infrastructures within the mainstream; promoting differentiation through transformation of the curriculum and pedagogy; and redefining the role of SENCOs (Clark et al. 1995a, Dyson et al. 1994, Dyson and Millward 2000).

The development of inclusive practices has seen some schools pushing back the boundaries of whole school approaches and exploring even further methods of enhancing teaching and learning for all pupils. This led Dyson and Millward (2000) (and Dyson et al. 1994) to note that in some schools:

> quite dramatic transformations were evident – schools which dismantled their special needs departments, abandoned all forms of segregated provision, reinvented their SENCOs as teaching and learning co-ordinators, embarked on intensive programmes of staff development, set up quality assurance programmes to enhance teaching and learning across the school and invested heavily in resource based learning in order to create flexible learning environments across the school.
>
> (Dyson and Millward 2000: 11)

> The inclusiveness of English schools has to be defined therefore not simply in terms of which students they educate, but in terms of how they educate them.
>
> (Dyson and Millward 2000: 11)

Consequently, inclusion is not about the mere presence of children with SEN, it has to lead to participation, be guided by notions of equity, and a fundamental recognition that the school system needs to adapt to meet the individual learning needs of the pupils it serves. In order to examine these changes in emphasis, Clark et al. (1995a) advocate that the practicality of inclusion, as well as the theoretical frameworks that underpin it, must be fully considered in order to arrive at a comprehensive appreciation of all the key issues of provision. This position is to some extent now being reflected in the 02/02 'Professional Standards Framework' (TTA 2002) in which both knowledge of SEN and inclusion is required, but significantly trainee teachers are expected to be able to demonstrate its application in order to meet the requirements for the award of QTS.

Moving towards an understanding of inclusion

It is recognised that in recent years (along with many other aspects of SEN terminology) we have become used to the terms inclusion, inclusive education and inclusive schools being used interchangeably (Dyson and Millward 2000,

Barton 1998, Depauw and Doll-Tepper 2000). In attempting to unpack the similarities and differences, it is relevant to note that within this chapter the complexities of inclusion need to be considered within a context that reflects government and statutory agencies, professional opinion and practice (teaching pedagogy) and consumer levels of classroom practice involving curriculum structure, experiences and outcomes. Thus Clark *et al.*'s (1995a, 1997) view of interpretation of theoretical and practical contexts is of particular relevance, and in considering this approach, Lipsky and Gartner suggest that 'while there is no single educational model or approach, inclusive schools tend to share similar characteristics and beliefs' (Lipsky and Gartner 1999: 17).

For example:

- **school-wide approaches** – in which the philosophy and practice of inclusive education is accepted by all the stakeholders;
- **all children learn together** – reflecting a continuum of learning needs within contexts of 'whole school approaches';
- **a sense of 'community' within schools** – through which children and teachers are valued (in addition, trainee teachers are required to demonstrate evidence of the promotion of positive values within the 02/02 (TTA 2002) 'Professional Standards Framework' (TTA 2002));
- **services based on need, rather than category** – recognising and responding to individual need as a starting point for supporting inclusive practice;
- **extensive teacher collaboration** – involving recognition of multi-agency working, and thus linking with the desire of the DfES *Schools Achieving Success* (2001a) publication to promote collaborative working;
- **curriculum adaptation** – through which inclusion provides adaptations to enable all pupils to benefit from a common school curriculum;
- **enhanced instructional strategies** – encouraged and developed within ITT and continuing professional development (CPD), then facilitated in practice by teachers in schools;
- **standards and outcomes** – linked and drawn from those expected of children in general.

Whilst Lipsky and Gartner's (1999) list helps to identify a number of important inclusive school factors, Dyson and Millward (2000) argue that it also poses many problems, with the belief that all stakeholders will accept a particular philosophy or set of inclusive practices. In reality these 'fly in the face of what we know about the complexity of school life' (Dyson and Millward 2000: 18). This contrasting view of the interrelationship of theory and practice is one of many offering schools guidance on how to become more inclusive and indicates the extent to which inclusive education is both complex and problematic to implement (Booth *et al.* 1998, Clark *et al.* 1995a, Porter 1997, Ainscow and Tweddle 1998, Rouse and Florian 1996, Thomas *et al.* 1998).

In attempting to draw perspectives together, Dyson (2001) argues that in order to understand what inclusion stands for in principle and practice, the detail of many authors' views is weak on underpinning theoretical frameworks, organisational structures and processes that lead to either inclusion or exclusion. Consequently, in order to arrive at a thorough appreciation of inclusion for children with SEN there is a need to examine the combined strengths of 'theoretical' and 'applied' views on inclusive practice. In Dyson's view this can best be achieved through a collective critique of two authors' work, namely 'Skrtic's theoretical models of inclusive practice' and 'Ainscow's examination of applied inclusive practice' in schools. Therefore in order to arrive at a coherent view of the fundamental principles, processes and practices concerned with inclusion, by examining the work of Skrtic and Ainscow a clearer picture should begin to emerge.

Skrtic's adhocratic schools

Skrtic (1991) argues from a position of 'crisis in modern knowledge', and a loss of confidence in the current state of special education understanding. He believes that in arriving at the inclusive standpoint of today, the profession has been subject to a range of sociological, philosophical and political critiques. From a sociological perspective, Skrtic suggests professionals operate in a manner that realises the interests of its members, within the context of the organisations in which they operate, and consequently impose their own constraints and imperatives to suit their, rather than children's, needs. In contrast, philosophical perspectives refer to a wide-ranging transformation in the way in which knowledge and certainty have come to be understood, and recognise there is not one paradigm through which knowledge is universally transferred. Skrtic indicates that interpretivist, radical humanist and radical structuralist paradigms have challenged the previously dominant functionalist paradigm of the 1960s, and as a direct consequence there are now many competing theories on special education (Pijl *et al.* 1997, Clark *et al.* 1995a, Clark *et al.* 1997, Dyson 2001).

Skrtic's political critique recognises that, in the past, the profession has argued from a position of access to privileged knowledge. However, this knowledge and understanding is now subject to scrutiny and questioning by competing theories, resulting in a diminishment of the power that they exercise over other people. In addition the emergence of agencies such as OFSTED and the TTA have contributed to the diminishing power base originally dominated solely by the teaching profession. In appreciation of the changing nature of inclusive education, Skrtic takes the view that special education is grounded in four assumptions:

- disabilities are pathological;
- differential diagnosis is objective and useful;
- special education is a rationally conceived and co-ordinated system of services that benefit diagnosed pupils;
- progress results from incremental technological improvement in diagnosis and instructional interventions (Skrtic 1995: 54).

The special education field cannot therefore be grounded in foundational knowledge, and this view complements the UK position in which many researchers (Tomlinson 1982, 1985, Oliver 1988, 1990, and Barton 1998) have indicated that disability has been constructed in a manner that serves the purposes of the profession rather than the client, and is subject to a range of views and opinions. This supports the earlier views of Pring (1996) and UCET (1997a) who note that many agencies and individuals have a role to play in determining what the nature of education, standards in ITT, and the Government's drive for 'school improvement' should consist of.

As a consequence, Skrtic suggests that whilst radical theorists claim to have changed the nature of SEN and inclusive provision, they have not sufficiently challenged the bureaucratic configuration of schools and the convergent thinking of the professional culture in a sufficiently fundamental manner (Skrtic 1995). Thus whilst there has been a call for the dismantling of separate special schools, the bureaucracy still establishes systems that do not sufficiently respond to diversity, and Skrtic (citing Mintzberg 1979, 1983) designates this as an 'adhocracy'.

In considering this 'adhocracy', Skrtic explains:

> The professional bureaucracy is non adaptable because it is premised on the principle of standardisation, which configures it as a performance organisation for perfecting standard (rather than flexible) programmes. An adhocracy is premised upon principles of innovation, rather than standardisation; as such, it is a problem-solving organisation configured to invent new programs. It is the organisational form that configures itself around work that is so ambiguous and uncertain that neither the programs nor the knowledge and skills for doing it are known.
>
> (Skrtic 1991: 182)

The adhocratic organisation has therefore many advantages in that, Skrtic argues, it encourages collaboration between professionals with different kinds of expertise; involves discursive coupling through which teams reflect upon practice; team approaches in which theory and practice are unified through informal communication; professional–political accountability and a community of common interests. As a result:

A school configured in this way would see the diversity of its students not as a disruption to be minimised by 'pigeonholing' the students into existing or separate programmes, but as a problem to be solved through a collaborative commitment to innovation.

(Dyson and Millward 2000: 25)

This supports the view of the TTA, who see teaching as a reflective-based profession and therefore this needs to be encouraged and fostered with trainee teachers as part of their ITT.

In summarising the adhocracy, Dyson and Millward (2000) suggest that Skrtic's views 'ultimately are philosophical rather than empirical. In particular they are grounded in the theory of knowledge rather than in studies of actual schools' (Dyson and Millward 2000: 27).

However, Skrtic argues that the empirical realties of schools are intentionally not addressed, in order that they do not interrupt the open and free flow of his thinking, rather than establish arguments around constraints of existing structures. Thus, it is for others to look to how the adhocratic models can be implemented structurally (official line) and delivered in practice (professional opinion and practice and impact on the consumers).

In response, Dyson and Millward (2000) cite the work of Ainscow, and his notion of 'the moving school' in which he documents 'good inclusive practice' in schools as an answer to the need to provide empirical substance to the inclusion debate. Consequently, Ainscow is concerned with documenting not only the good practice but also, more significantly, what, why and how it is deemed to be good inclusive practice. As a result, Ainscow's documented practice is grounded in wider circumstances of institutional development, professional development and special education.

Ainscow's documentation of inclusive school practice

Ainscow defines inclusion as:

a process of increasing the participation of pupils in, and reducing their exclusion from, the cultures, curricula and communities of their local schools, not forgetting, of course, that education involves many processes that occur outside of schools.

(Ainscow 1999: 218)

He suggests inclusion is often viewed as involving movement from special to mainstream contexts under a belief that once there they will be 'included'. Inclusion should, however, be considered 'as a never ending process, rather than a simple change of state, and as dependent on continuous pedagogical and organisational development within the mainstream' (Ainscow 1999: 218).

This view is of particular interest to Dyson and Millward (2000), as Ainscow links pedagogical development to teacher development, and then assimilates this to the organisational development of schools. This standpoint is at the centre of Ainscow's model of inclusive practice in which he advocates a desire to move away from views of locating the problem with the child, and look to an examination of curriculum adaptation and modification (social model). Consequently, inadequacies of learning environments should be seen as generating the learning difficulty, rather than the individual characteristics (medical model) of the pupil (Ainscow 1994). In order to develop the theme of curricula, rather than pupil adaptation, Ainscow (1999) believes that schools must become 'moving schools', which are in a constant state of inclusive development and change in order to adapt to the individual needs of all its pupils. Schools should therefore be looking to develop their inclusive practice around a number of core areas, namely:

- **effective leadership** – incorporating a clear vision and strategy for making inclusive practice work;
- **involvement of all staff, students and the community** – and this supports notions of citizenship in the National Curriculum (2000) in which all people understand their rights and responsibilities to respect and value diversity;
- **commitment to collaborative planning** – in which, through multi-agency working, children with SEN receive an holistic approach to their education;
- **attention to the benefits of enquiry and reflection** – supporting teachers as reflective practitioners, constantly prepared to modify and adapt their teaching and learning approaches;
- **policies for staff development that focus on classroom practice** – through which all staff are offered opportunities for continuing professional development to enhance their knowledge and understanding.

The fundamental premise of inclusive school practice is designed therefore to support Ainscow's notion of a changing school, responding flexibly to the individual need of its pupils, rather than the other way around in which children have to adapt to fit pre-existing educational settings. As a result of the notions of constantly changing schools, Dyson and Millward (2000) argue that due to the empirical basis of Ainscow's views there is significant credence in supporting his models of inclusive practice in schools. Consequently ITT needs to be constructed within a framework of creating reflective teachers who are responsive and adaptable to the individual needs of pupils that they serve in schools.

Common themes – an inclusive approach to teaching children with SEN

The work of Skrtic and Ainscow has made significant contributions toward articulated theoretical accounts of the relationship between principles and processes of inclusive practice and school organisation (Lloyd 2000, Dyson and Millward 2000, Dyson 2001, Fredrickson and Cline 2002). Within this context, attempts have been made to identify 'common themes' that have emerged in schools with reference to inclusive principles and practices, whilst identifying potential threats to this movement. Thus, whilst classes and schools may be very different in their approaches, it is possible (Dyson and Millward 2000) to establish characteristics of a 'model of the inclusive school', which can then be used as a basis for all the key stakeholders to work towards the creation of inclusive schools. In reflecting on the work of Skrtic and Ainscow, inclusive schools can be characterised by:

- **effective leadership** – in which all people in positions of responsibility (whether that be at Government, ITT or school level) drive forward the belief of inclusive practice;
- **clear vision** – in which all stakeholders work together to promote inclusive practice;
- **dismantling of structures and barriers** – through which agencies and individuals are prepared to review, modify and change policies and practices whether they be physical, attitudinal or financial barriers and constraints;
- **response to diversity** – in which difference is valued as an essential component of the make up of schools and wider society;
- **senior management responsibility** – in which people in positions of responsibility ensure that the visions of inclusive practice become a reality;
- **reliance on in-class support** – in contrast to separate or segregated provision;
- **emphasis on the professional development of staff** – as the future of inclusive provision rests with the skills, expertise and determination of staff to make inclusive practice a reality for children with SEN.

Conclusion and future directions in inclusion for children with SEN

Dyson and Millward (2000) argue that through a combination of Ainscow's and Skrtic's inclusive models, and their own case studies of common themes lending empirical weight, an 'illuminating explanation' (Dyson and Millward 2000: 149) of the nature of inclusive education for children with SEN begins

Task 2.4 Characteristics of inclusive schools

Review your understanding of the similarities and differences between Skirtic's adhocratic schools and Ainscow's documentation of inclusive practice and what you see as the implications for teaching children with SEN in PE. Once you have done this, use the table below to look at the common theme of inclusive practice and reflect upon what you understand by each aspect and its relationship to teaching children with SEN in PE.

Characteristics of inclusive schools	Your understanding of the aspect	Relationship to teaching children with SEN in PE
Effective leadership: all people in positions of responsibility drive forward the belief of inclusive practice		
Clear vision: all stakeholders work together to promote inclusive practice		
Dismantling of structures and barriers: agencies and individuals are prepared to review, modify and change policies and practices		
Response to diversity: difference is valued as an essential component of the make up of schools		
Senior management responsibility: people in positions of responsibility ensure visions of inclusive practice become a reality		

Reliance on in-class support: in contrast to separate or segregated provision		
Emphasis on the professional development of staff: future of inclusive provision rests with the skills, expertise and determination of staff		

to emerge. Thus, in taking account of 'the multiple values' (Norwich 2002a: 484) offered by the authors above, a clearer picture on the nature of training required to equip teachers of PE begins to emerge.

In support of a clearer picture emerging on the nature of inclusive practice, Reynolds *et al.* (2000) notes that two paradigms have dominated school improvement over recent years, and consequently have assisted with the development of teaching and learning approaches for children with SEN. The first is concerned with a 'top-down process', which is centrally designed, through which innovation and change is transmitted to schools. In contrast, the 'bottom-up process' involves building upon the professional development of teachers and involving them fully in the development of school improvement and inclusive practice. Dyson and Millward (2000) additionally suggest that the development of educational policy 'cannot simply be seen as a technical-rational process of formulation and implementation' (Dyson and Millward 2000: 157).

Dyson and Millward (2000) state that educational progress is fraught with conflict, contest and compromise out of which may come policy positions that are far from coherent. In contexts of top down and bottom up change processes, therefore, and the nature of conflict, it is easy to appreciate why apparently well intentioned models of inclusion, integration or whole school approaches for children with SEN seem often to deliver less than they initially promise (Lloyd 2000, Croll and Moses 2000). This conflicting picture:

> has illuminated the way in which such policies, both in formation and in practice, are shaped by, inter alia, ambiguous and contradictory national imperatives, interacting with the competing interests of head teachers, parents and others with a vested interest in the nature of that provision.
>
> (Dyson and Millward 2000: 157)

School improvement, and inclusive theories and practices, become ever more complex and problematic to disentangle (Rouse and Florian 1997, Vincent *et al.* 1994, Visle and Langfeldt 1996). As a result, Feiler and Gibson (1999) argue that within this background there are four potential threats to the inclusion movement, which need to be addressed as a matter of urgency prior to any further developments in relation to the education of children with SEN, which are:

- a lack of consistency in the definition and understanding of inclusion;
- a lack of empirical data;
- notions of internal exclusion (i.e. streaming or grouping);
- a tendency to describe individual needs in a manner that implies the problem resides with the child, rather than the school structure.

In reflecting upon these four threats, the future development of special needs education needs to move towards a coherent framework within which government policy is reflected, delivered and implemented within a structure that ensures all agencies and individuals are clear about what the vision of inclusive schooling involves. In summary, with regard to future visions, Dyson (2001) succinctly makes the following statements, which act as a point for further reflection: 'Special needs education so patently has a past and that past – like the present – is highly fluid and even turbulent' (Dyson 2001: 24). In coming to terms with the future:

> It is my contention that the inherent instability of the present means that it is incumbent on us to look carefully at what the future might hold. Even as the 'new' resolution of 'inclusion' struggles to establish its hegemony, we should, I believe, try to understand how it will ultimately fragment and what possibilities might open up for alternative resolutions.
>
> (Dyson 2001: 27)

Chapter 3

Movement, learning and ranges of special educational need

Introduction

Children with SEN, like their non-disabled peers, need to experience physical movement, learning and development in a wide range of activities and environments as part of their education. The rationale for supporting the development of children's movement patterns is twofold: first for their own physical development, and second it can be seen as an essential aspect of their social, emotional, intellectual and cognitive development.

For children, physical activity and movement enhances fitness, fosters growth and development, and helps teach them about their world. As teachers of young children, we know that most children are innately physically active and that they learn as they move around their environment. Consequently, in observing children at break times, we often see them running, jumping, throwing, and playing in informal and unstructured settings.

However, in today's modern age of computers, concerns over child safety and longer working hours for parents, young people often find themselves involved in sedentary alternatives (see Fairclough and Stratton 2005). For example, children tend to ride in a car or bus to school, have less PE, watch more television, play more sedentary games, and do not have as much freedom to play outside on their own. Consequently, there is mounting evidence that even the youngest of children are becoming less physically active and more overweight and obese. This is contributing to an increased prevalence of childhood obesity and other risk factors which have resulted in the production of a *Healthy Living Blueprint for Schools* (DfES 2004b, 0781) which suggests schools and teachers should promote a school ethos and environment which encourages a healthy lifestyle and:

- use the full capacity of the curriculum to achieve a healthy lifestyle;
- ensure that the food and drink across the school day reinforces the healthy lifestyle message;
- provide high quality physical education and school sport, and promote physical activity as part of a lifelong healthy lifestyle;

- promote an understanding of the full range of issues and behaviours which impact upon lifelong learning.

Whilst the comments above establish the generalised picture for young people, what is of particular concern to this chapter and the book is the movement and physical activity levels of children with SEN. Thus whilst all of the issues and concerns raised with regard to sedentary physical activity are equally applied to children with SEN, what is often the case is that as a consequence of their disabilities this can be compounded even further and immobility for whatever reasons can lead to increased weight, therefore making movement progressively harder. This chapter sets out to examine the fundamental principles of learning and movement before proceeding to an overview of the range of SEN that teachers are likely to be presented with in school. As with other chapters, the purpose of providing detailed overviews of children with SEN is in order for teachers to review existing practices and be fully prepared to modify and adapt teaching and learning activities to maximise opportunities for positive PE experiences.

Learning to move, moving to learn

There is considerable awareness of the contribution that PE lessons have on the physical, social, emotional and intellectual development of all children. However, PE has an even greater role to play in the overall growth and development of the vast majority of pupils with SEN. The relevance and importance of learning through physical activity cannot be overstated. In relation to PE a SEN can be attributed to any child who has a movement difficulty, which in reality involves a broad range of pupils. However, in addition to this rather generalised statement there are many groups of children who can easily be recognised as having a SEN in PE. These include:

- sensory impairments (both visual and auditory);
- locomotion and other movement problems;
- severe or moderate learning difficulties;
- medical conditions such as diabetes, epilepsy or asthma;
- emotional and behavioural disorders;
- profound and multiple learning difficulties.

Many of these conditions can lead to a lack of confidence in body management which in turn leads to difficulties in gaining positive experiences in PE and this is where the teacher is vital to the process of ensuring children with SEN do not feel disadvantaged. Furthermore, it is important that PE for children with SEN is not seen purely in a physical light, as many activities present additional opportunities to develop social skills that can lead to a free and independent life in a context that is relevant, real, pleasurable and creative. An exciting PE programme can stimulate and motivate pupils who in turn are less likely to become frustrated or emotionally disturbed, and consequently children with SEN should be given every opportunity and encouraged to use these opportunities to the best of their ability.

The aims of PE for pupils with SEN are no different from those of any other child, in that they are entitled to a broad, balanced, progressive, differentiated and relevant programme of activities. Clearly, some children will have greater difficulties than others in terms of active participation, but it is important that provision be made for their inclusion alongside their non-disabled peers. It is also important to note that, should it be necessary for an activity or equipment to be modified or substituted, it maintains its educational integrity. Pupils with SEN by their very nature are individuals who possess a wide range of personal and specific needs which have enormous complexity and diversity. To offer a comprehensive programme in PE will present considerable challenges for teachers and schools and the task therefore lies in the identification of individual needs and provision of a range of activities to satisfy these needs. The skills learnt and experiences shared will support them and carry them forward into adult life and assist them towards an active and worthwhile role within the community. The teacher's reward is to see each pupil develop and attain their full potential.

What are movement patterns and motor development?

Any movement pattern can be described as a definite arrangement of muscle actions which are required to achieve a desired outcome. For example, throwing a ball, turning around or jumping in the air are all distinctive movement patterns. Movement patterns can be likened to general templates that then become the basis for a number of specific skills such as those used in gymnastics, dance or games activities. Thus an underarm throw can be described as a movement pattern, whilst a bowl in rounders or a pass in netball can be seen as specific skills which develop from it. Furthermore, a turn of the whole body is seen as a movement pattern whilst a spin in dance or turn in gymnastics are referred to as specific skills which develop from it.

It is vital for all children that basic movement patterns are established before progression to specialised skill development. Most movement patterns become established during the early years of child development provided they have had sufficient stimulus and opportunity to utilise them. Whilst some children may need more encouragement than others to practice and apply them in different situations, usually by the age of around seven most children will have sound templates of movement patterns. However, for some children with SEN this achievement may take much longer and require significant intervention, adaptation and support.

The establishment of sound basic movement patterns allows children to progress by building upon these templates and combining and refining them to specific situations and developing specialist skills. PE offers an opportunity to support this development, particularly in primary school in the Foundation and Key Stage One phases. This supports the requirement of the PE NC 2000 to establish the foundations for future skill development and establishment of basic movement patterns. These can be seen as the foundations of all future physical learning and PE teachers in these early stages should focus more on learning generalised movement patterns rather than specific skill development, which can be focused upon at a later stage.

Supporting children to develop and learn motor skills

The dual processes of learning and development are responsible for much of what we observe in children's skill. These are stimulated by qualities such as motivation and persistence, although development and learning are central to what a child offers and receives in the PE setting. These concepts, although different, are also difficult to separate, with developments being a combination of maturation and the interrelationship with everyday experiences and learning. Clearly these will be different according to the phase of development a child is at, although by teachers examining these processes it helps to provide a better foundation and understanding of children's functioning which in turn will contribute towards ensuring they have positive PE experiences.

Although there are no distinctive stages in a child's motor development, there are global phases the child passes through from birth to maturity. As a result it is important to consider these phases from birth because many children with SEN will show movement characteristics of children who are much younger. Whilst age in years and months is not a totally accurate guide to development because of individual differences, it does offer some comparability to make judgements about children and SEN. This is particularly true with children with SEN whose developmental progress can vary dramatically from those who are in normal ranges, and may continue to remain delayed even in later childhood.

From birth to two years of age

During this period children develop rapidly and acquire three basic skills of **locomotion, posture** and **manipulation**. Posture can be seen as the precursor to locomotion and involves the control of various parts of the body, such as the head and trunk, whilst lying and sitting prior to eventual progression to an upright stance. In some children with SEN who have profound and/ or multiple learning difficulties, these developmental progressions may provide the basis for targets and learning activities during PE lessons. One of the key milestones in any child's development is progression to upright locomotion, which typically occurs around one year of age but varies significantly with children with SEN. From a child's first steps they use this newfound skill in a number of environmental contexts leading to complex locomotor activities that we seek to present and develop in our PE lessons. Again the variations of upright locomotion usually found in the first two years of life can provide opportunities for children of all ages. Manipulation progresses steadily in the first two years, with reaching becoming more accurate and grasping changing from crude palmed responses to delicate pincer grips involving the thumb and first finger. In PE reaching for and grasping objects of different sizes, shapes, weights, colours and textures can provide the foundation stones for many activities. Therefore, if necessary, progression can be used by PE teachers to present movement situations to children in their lessons which accommodate the particular stage of development that they are at.

Task 3.1 Defining key terms

Reflect on your understanding of the terms locomotion, posture and manipulation and consider their relationship to PE and the type of activities you can employ to support and enhance their development.

From age two through to seven years of age

During this period children develop all the basic locomotor skills alongside self-help skills. For example, by the age of six or seven most children can run, jump, hop, skip, throw, climb, catch, kick, stride out, dress, wash, produce recognisable letters and shapes and perform everyday manipulation skills. Whilst children may not be able to do all of these to a highly accomplished level, most will be able to execute them in a rudimentary fashion. However, some children with SEN will either be delayed or have great difficulty in executing these and this may again be a fundamental focus for work and support within PE lessons. When a child with SEN has difficulty with these tasks it can occur for variety of reasons. For example it may be due to a child not experiencing the full range of everyday daily living experiences that are normally associated with standard child development. If this is the case the child may enter pre-school or school without the necessary skills, but then may quickly gain them with exposure to the right type of activities within PE lessons. It is desirable for children at this stage of development to have a vocabulary and motor skills vocabulary which allow them to be more flexible and utilise these in variety of situations rather than go down a route of exacting specific and highly defined tasks. However, whilst some children will progress rapidly once they enter school, others (especially those with SEN) will continue to pose challenges for teachers.

Therefore any PE or movement-based programme should incorporate a diverse range of skills rather than seek depth, in order to provide the basis for more specific skills that will appear later. It is also during this period of development that natural progression of locomotor skills takes place. For example, in relation to jumping the first jump is often a step down from one foot to the other, followed by a two-foot take-off from the ground. A two-foot standing long jump follows this, with alterations to arm and body positions, before mature jumping skills are perfected. It is also worth noting that jumping occurs before hopping, which in turn starts before skipping.

Differences between boys and girls are not significant at these phases, although boys tend to be superior in ball skills whilst girls are superior at rhythmic co-ordination such as hopping and skipping tasks. Towards the end of this phase, studies have found greater incidence of clumsiness in boys than in girls which is worth noticing and being ready for as part of the planning process for PE lessons.

Age seven years through to puberty

It is at this phase of motor development that children do not acquire new fundamental skills. Rather, what they are doing is going through a process of refining, honing and elaborating upon the skills they have already gained and now begin to adapt them to new situations, make them more elegant, use them in a variety of contexts, and respond to changing environmental demands. Consequently, children who were competent at controlling movements now progress to situations where they need to become competent with others rather than just themselves. By the age of seven they have control of their own bodies but are generally not good at responding and reacting to environmental demands. Children before age seven do not have spontaneous responses to situations which demand that they respond to moving environments, such as running to strike a moving ball. It is at this stage where individual differences become more noticeable and particularly where distinctions can become significant and more apparent in children with SEN alongside their non-disabled peers.

The natural development in children has significant implications for PE, especially at the primary phase when tasks are presented in varying contexts with different people and social groupings. Therefore, it is critical that PE activities are structured in a manner that allows children to make spatial and temporal decisions often at speed. Children from seven through to puberty are developing perceptually and cognitively, and development in these carries over into the motor domain. Children show great expectation, for example in anticipation and predictive skills that are crucial to playing games activities, whilst additionally requiring responses to others in fast-moving environments. In relation to children with SEN it can be considered even more important because many of their needs are much more complex and involve other interacting areas in addition to motor skills. For example, perceptual and cognitive systems may not be as developed and situations that involve prediction and anticipation may need to be simplified. It is here that gender differences can become present, whereby boys tend to continue to be proficient at ball skills and are up to a year ahead in running, speed and jumping distances. In contrast, girls continue to show superior ability in rhythmic and co-ordinated activities whilst showing lower incidences of motor difficulties and delay.

From puberty through to adulthood

This phase brings great physical changes in a person's capacity, with children becoming bigger, stronger and having greater physical capability. It is also at this stage that children begin to choose which activities to take part in as part of school sport or physical activity and leisure outside of school. It is worth noting here, though, that increases in strength are often compensated for by a lack of skill at this stage so it is vital for children to be presented with skilful learning situations in PE which continue to enable them to participate recreationally as well as part of the PE curriculum. There is also significant variability in the onset of puberty, which can start as young as nine in some girls and be as late as fifteen in boys. Boys tend to go through puberty for a longer period of time and change occurs at greater intensities. Consequently boys who are at the post-puberty stage tend to be as a group better at power, strength and endurance activities. However, on tasks which require pure skilled movements there is no significant gender difference. These differences offer children with SEN opportunities to experience different types of activity depending on their specific needs. However, it is necessary to show some degree of caution in that children with severe learning difficulties may be going through puberty biologically, yet socially, emotionally and cognitively may be functioning at a much lower level. This kind of developmental profile has significant implications and raises issues that require consideration in relation to the nature and manner within which tasks are presented in PE lessons.

The learning process in PE

When children attempt to learn a new task the first operation is the need to **understand the skill**, with teachers simultaneously knowing how to get children into the skill in the first instance and how to get them to understand what is demanded of them and the resources they need to meet that demand. This is a critical aspect of the learning process and one that is sometimes overlooked. As a result if teachers do overlook this part, the rest of the learning process (especially in relation to SEN) cannot be fully successful. Consequently during this part of the learning process it is vital that teachers offer demonstrations, instructions and explanations which bring clarity to the situations that are being presented to them.

The second aspect of the learning process involves **acquiring and refining skills**, whereby the child knows what to do and is now involved in the actual physical process of learning and development. During this aspect of learning teachers need to point out what is right and help with aspects that need refinement and correction. As a teacher, observational skills are vital here in order to provide immediate and constructive feedback to children. The third part is **automatising these skills**, where the child becomes quite competent and performs without paying much attention to it. Another aspect which permeates across all stages is **generalising the skill**, involving children using the skills learned so far to help them with a new skill that has been presented to them. Whilst these skills will overlap with each other it is not useful to try to make definitive distinctions at this stage, whilst observational skills in teachers are again vital here.

In PE lessons teachers are involved in a series of activities that stimulate the learning process, which involve:

- providing instructions and explanations;
- giving demonstrations;
- providing appropriate practices and giving timely feedback.

Task 3.2 The four elements of the learning process
Use the table below to reflect on four elements of the learning process in PE. You should consider your understanding of each of the terms and its relationship to PE, whilst additionally considering any implications for teaching children with SEN.

Aspect of the learning process	Your interpretation and its relationship to PE	Considerations related to children with SEN
Understanding the skill		
Acquiring and refining the skill		
Automatising the skill		
Generalising the skill		

Whilst the above is not the total sum of the teaching process, they do take a significant proportion of a teacher's time. The issue for you as a teacher becomes one of how the teaching activities change through the different learning phases that children pass through. Whilst absolute protocols cannot be provided, there are guidelines to consider and reflect upon as part of your planning of PE lessons. For example, when a child is first learning a new skill, instructions need to be short and very clear, with the objective of getting the child into the task as quickly as possible. Here feedback is essential and needs to be short and explicit, with practice engaging children in simple activities. As the child acquires and refines the skill, instructions and feedback can become more detailed; although practice needs to focus on one or two aspects, it can become more varied. In children with SEN it may be necessary to spend longer on certain aspects of tasks. For example, children with learning difficulties often have problems getting into the task. Once they are doing it they are fine, but getting to that point can be problematic for them and for you as a teacher, and can test your ingenuity, flexibility and adaptation and modification skills. As a result, more time may need to be spent in ensuring a child with SEN understands what is required, and this may involve extensive elaboration and further explanation.

The ranges of SEN

The first point to make in any discussion on ranges of SEN is that not all children will have difficulties in PE lessons. For example, a child with emotional and behavioural difficulties could excel in gymnastics or a child with learning difficulties may be an excellent swimmer. Consequently we should not assume that SEN equals difficulty. However, SEN pupils are going to pose challenges for you as the teacher and this is where having an open mind, high expectations and a willingness to adapt your practices are critical to successful PE experiences. This part of the chapter will now provide you with a range of characteristics of children with SEN, but it is important to stress this is not a definitive list, and it is essential that you continue to recognise and value the uniqueness of each child. Consequently, developing strategies for consultation and flexibility should remain a constant focus for your practice. Thus the following overview on ranges of SEN should merely act as a starting point for your reflection, and not an end point.

The adaptation of practices and/or lack of access to PE for a child with SEN are particularly well reinforced in the statement by Fredrickson and Cline (2002: 40) who suggest, 'at one extreme then, the environmentally focused approach holds that there are no students with learning difficulties, only adults with teaching difficulties'. Consequently the requirement to modify and adapt practices (reinforced through the PE NC 2000) suggests that any barriers or lack of success in many aspects will come down to you as the teacher and not generally be any fault of the child's. As a result, it is essential that we start from the premise that all children can learn and develop if the right opportunities are provided for them.

What you need to do as the teacher is examine the interrelated dynamics of the teacher, the environment, and the individual needs of the child which can all be considered as essential ingredients in the success or lack of PE lessons for children with SEN. According to Sugden and Keogh (1990), any outcome in PE is a result of three interacting variables which are:

- the resources the child brings to the learning situation;
- the context within which learning takes place (teacher);
- the task to be performed.

Thus children have certain ranges of movement that need to be considered fully by the teacher in order to provide a successful outcome. What you need to do as the teacher is ensure that selection and breakdown of the task is appropriate in order to achieve a successful result. Finally, the environmental context can make or break the success of the child, which involves you, the teaching space and the other pupils within the class.

Task 3.3 Three interacting variables of teaching and learning
Reflect on the three interacting variables noted by Sugden and Keogh (1990) and examine the strategies you would employ to ensure positive outcomes in PE for children with SEN.

It is often the case that children with SEN are classified according to the severity of their particular conditions. However, whilst this can initially appear to be logical, it is not the most useful or productive point from which to progress forward. For example, there are some children with severe conditions who only require minimal adaptations, whilst others with fewer and less complex needs require significant intervention. The other issue to note here relates to a requirement upon you to take a social model approach and consider what you need to do to fit your teaching and learning environment around the child, rather than the other way around. Consequently the descriptions below illustrate some of the characteristics of children with SEN whilst still recognising that children with these conditions can have very different needs and responses to PE, movement and learning.

Children with specific movement difficulties

In any statement of SEN, or in earlier stages of the Code of Practice, children with specific movement difficulties are recognised for their needs in the movement domain and usually have medical conditions that supplement these. It is important again to recognise that the potential for a positive outcome is great and you as the teacher need to establish high expectations, an open mind and a commitment to modify and adapt practices as necessary.

Cerebral palsy covers a range of conditions which manifest themselves through poor motor control as a result of damage to the brain. Whilst children with cerebral palsy do not notably experience deterioration in their condition, changes do take place which make diagnosis a little unstable. The damage is usually early in childhood and the most significant impact is impairment of movement accompanied by other related difficulties. Many children with cerebral palsy may also have general learning, speech and language difficulties. Cerebral palsy is classified in a number of ways, but teachers are most likely to see it described through the characteristics noted below. A child's cerebral palsy is usually referred to as mild, moderate or severe. However, this is not the total picture as children are also classified according to the location of their impairment. For example, we have terms like **quadriplegia** (all four limbs are affected), **hemiplegia** (one side involved, or one side involved more than the other), **diplegia** (legs only affected, or more so than the arms).

The third aspect of classification examines the types of movement that a child performs, which are commonly referred to as **spasticity**, involving muscle tone, build-up of tension and releasing movements. The often noticeable rigid tonus is not always present, and can vary according to emotional states and which part of the body is involved. Abnormal reflexes are typical of all types of cerebral palsy and in spasticity the child has great difficulty in breaking free of the movements imposed upon them by their reflexes. This is compounded through involuntary control by the increased hyperconicity, which in some cases can be so severe that it can fixate the limbs in a few typical postures. In addition, when working with children with cerebral palsy you are often likely to see what is referred to as a 'scissor gait', which is presented by flexion of the hip, knee and ankle and rotation of the leg towards the midline, creating balance and locomotion difficulties.

The second major type of cerebral palsy is referred to as **athetosis**, which involves fluctuating muscle tone, often resulting in what looks like seemingly purposeless and uncontrollable movements; children may display writhing, squirming and swiping movements. These fluctuations in muscle control can make it difficult for children to maintain a stable posture, and this is heightened by muscle spasms, flexion and extension. The situation is often compounded further by athetoid and spastic movements that result in lack of head control, which can impact upon visual tracking activities in PE.

Ataxia is another form of cerebral palsy, and is characterised by postural instability and problems in balance and co-ordination which show when children sit, walk and stand. There is usually poor fixation of the head and trunk, and this promotes a stumbling gait whereby movements appear clumsy.

It is important to recognise that children with cerebral palsy can take part in PE, and play an active part in these lessons. The key to creating successful PE experiences for such children is in appreciating the issues and needs discussed above, and your response to the challenges they pose to your teaching and learning.

Spina bifida is part of a group of conditions in which formation of the neural tube is compromised. The higher the site of damage, the more disabling the condition. Prevalence has been estimated at between 1 and 3 per 1,000, and children have a range of abilities from those requiring a wheelchair to those who are ambulant. There may also be some difficulties with fine motor movements and perceptual difficulties, and some children may be incontinent, which requires management.

Muscular dystrophy is part of a subgroup of conditions caused by disorders of the neuromuscular system, and is characterised by wasting and progressive weakness of the muscles. It is different from the other conditions described above in that the physical condition deteriorates over time, although teaching and therapy can help to slow down the process. Children with muscular dystrophy will need careful monitoring, planning and emotional support.

Children with **brittle bones** have a predisposition to bone fractures, caused by a lack of the protein collagen which gives strength to bones and ligaments. This can be potentially hazardous, but through considered discussion with parents and medical staff they can still have positive PE experiences. Other conditions, such as cystic fibrosis, diabetes, asthma, epilepsy and haemophilia also impact on children's movement. If you are interested in finding out more about the characteristics of such conditions you can refer to the work of Winnick (2000) (see Further Reading, page 119).

Children with general movement difficulties

Children who lack the movement skills necessary to function effectively in PE lessons, yet have no identifiable neurological disorder, are fairly common in schools. They tend to exhibit delayed performances with movement skills, which can generally be described as at functionally low levels. Terms used to describe these children have included **clumsiness, clumsy child syndrome** and **dyspraxia**. However the most recent and widely recognised term has come to be known as **Development Co-ordination Disorder (DCD)**. Children with DCD acquire the basic skills of sitting, standing and walking but these may be delayed, and they usually have difficulty in demonstrating the flexibility to adapt to changing environmental conditions. They can usually perform skills at rather rudimentary levels but are less skilled than their peers, often have difficulty using skills in context and their movement patterns look rather awkward. This can lead to a lack of participation in PE and other leisure and play activities.

PE is not the only subject in which DCD is present and poses challenges for children, as most aspects of the NC require a basic level of motor competence. For example, in studies by Sugden and Henderson (1994) children with DCD have been identified as having problems with activities such as pouring, weighing, cutting, drawing and writing. Furthermore, they may also present with social, emotional and behavioural problems due to the difficulties they have with their movement.

The incidence of DCD varies, but research tends to suggest that around 5 per cent of children aged 5 to 11 years of age may have DCD, which results in around one or two children per class requiring support. Most studies have found incidence of DCD to be higher in boys, with the condition not having any fixed boundaries or clear characteristics but with a clear expectation that teachers will be required to modify and adapt their PE lessons. Research has shown that DCD is a condition that children do not grow out of, and this has been exemplified in studies where children with poor motor skills at six years of age still exhibit movement difficulties when re-tested ten years later. However, those who do improve tend to have had specific PE programmes that have worked on supporting their specific movement needs. Consequently, if children with DCD are left to their own devices they generally do not improve, and this may go on to affect other aspects of their social, physical, emotional and behavioural functioning both in and outside of school. On the other hand, children with DCD movement skills who undertake structured and specific intervention programmes that are managed in conjunction with occupational therapists, physiotherapists and PE teachers have shown significant improvement.

Children with learning difficulties

There are groups of children in schools (whether mainstream or special) who are not recognised for their physical disabilities, nor are they classified as clumsy or having DCD, yet they still have generalised movement difficulties as part of their overall profile. These children are referred to in the UK as **children with learning difficulties**, and they are usually identified in relation to their functional needs and difficulties in school subjects. In other counties IQ scores are used to group children along a continuum from mild through moderate to severe and profound, and in the USA these children are referred to as having mental retardation. In the UK we tend to group children through a range from mild to moderate, severe and profound and in addition there are identifiable sub groups such as **Down syndrome**.

There is a higher incidence of motor difficulties among children who are classed as having moderate learning difficulties, and as the severity of learning increases so does the incidence of motor difficulties. However, it is important to stress that some children with moderate learning difficulties will have no motor difficulties and will perform well, and even excel, in PE. As a result, as stressed on many occasions previously it is important to look at the individual needs of each child and consult with parents and support workers rather than make generalisations. This will involve you having to reflect on learning activities such as task adaptation, breaking down of tasks into smaller components and consideration of levels and degrees of feedback.

Children with sensory difficulties

Children with sensory difficulties in relation to being **blind** or **deaf** as a group also tend to have movement difficulties and will pose some challenges for teachers in PE lessons. For example, a child who has a loss of vision will find that this will impact upon their movement abilities, and you as a teacher will need to give consideration to the organisation of spatial information. In most children with visual difficulties vision is likely to be to some extent impaired rather than not present at all. This is where the need for teachers to consult with the individual child, parents and support workers is critical to a successful and positive outcome in PE.

As children who are blind grow up they tend to have difficulty with everyday tasks such as walking, riding a bike, running and general skill confidence. Therefore children asked to walk, jog or sprint in PE may need a lot of support, especially in relation to their involvement with other children in the class. Consequently the need for internal maps of the environment is critical, especially as vision is such a rich resource in PE for spatial awareness, observation of movement of self and others that it can leave such children with significant difficulties. These pupils may need the support of a teaching assistant to help them build their confidence.

Children who are **deaf** also require modification of their PE lessons and generally present with movement difficulties. They have specific needs, especially as they are cut off from the environment of your own and fellow pupils' world of sound. This will necessitate specific interventions on the part of the teacher and it will also have an impact on their learning of language. Some deaf children will have conductive hearing loss, which involves the transmission of sound through vibrations to the inner ear, whilst others have sensory neural damage which hinders perceptual information systems. Deafness tends to be identified on a number of dimensions, such as intensity and quality of sound, and it is vital that prior to any adaptation of PE activities you are clear about what the specific needs of each child are.

There is some evidence to show that children who have inner ear problems have some difficulties in balance, but this generally tends to not be a major issue and rather it is the challenges in relation to presentation and communication of tasks that need most consideration. The onus is therefore on you as the teacher to either be competent in sign language or have support in activities that require significant communication. Feedback, explanation, directions and demonstrations are also important and will need careful consideration in order to ensure successful PE experiences.

Children with emotional and behavioural difficulties

Children who fall into this grouping range from those who are withdrawn and reclusive through to those who are overly active, lack concentration, appear intentionally aggressive, destructive and even violent. The Elton Report from 1989 suggests that the main types of emotional and behavioural problems in school are those which are described as low intensity–high frequency. That is, the behaviour is not particularly serious but it happens regularly and impacts on the child concerned, other pupils and the teacher.

It is important not to see behavioural problems in isolation from the context within which they take place, and consequently the teacher and the school can determine the nature and degree of incidence. In any PE lesson the teacher has control of the context within which learning takes place and factors such as rules, rewards, punishments and how they are applied are critical. Consequently, blame should not be seen as an issue for extensive debate but rather the focus should be what needs to be organised in order to ensure that the nature of intervention and support for the individual children concerned is consistent and sufficiently decisive that both pupil and teacher know what the ground rules are.

Children with other needs

In discussing the range of needs found amongst children with SEN there will always be children who do not neatly fit into any category, and nor should they. There are children whose characteristics are idiosyncratic and yet they overlap with problems and difficulties already noted earlier in this chapter. For example, children with **attention deficit disorder (with or without hyperactivity) (ADHD)** have great difficulty in attending to relevant information, are easily distracted, and have short attention spans which can be accompanied by excessive motor activity and/or hyperactivity. Intervention for these children ranges from medication through to diet, behaviour modification and educational programmes.

For those children who struggle with attention spans PE can offer many activities that require short periods of concentration, such as performing gymnastic and dance routines. This, along with interventions elsewhere in the child's schooling, can go a significant way to improving this condition. In relation to behavioural difficulties, encouraging children to take leadership roles and to conform to rules and regulations can help support them with understanding their particular difficulties. Furthermore, research shows that the most important aspect of supporting such children is a consistent approach to the child's management and support, both within and outside of school. Professionals such as educational psychologists will often play a part in establishing behavioural support systems.

Autism and **Asperger's syndrome** are two further conditions which are more commonly noted by teachers in PE. Autism involves a number of needs, including language and communication skills, social and personal skills and stereotypical rhythmic activities. These contribute to posing many challenges for teachers in whatever aspect of schooling they are involved. Asperger's syndrome is a condition that is closely related to autism but these children tend to have improved cognitive and language skills; however, there is evidence that they tend to be clumsy with their motor skills.

Conclusion

In reflecting upon all the characteristics and ranges of SEN described within this chapter it is hoped that the key message that comes over is that children are individual, unique human beings. As a result, whilst the information offered in this chapter will help you with some initial ideas and thoughts it in no way intends to replace the need for consultation, negotiation and flexibility with the child and all those who support them. PE can be a highly positive experience for all children, whatever their range of needs and characteristics. The key for you is to have an open mind and seize the opportunity to be challenged to think creatively to support the children you work with.

Chapter 4

The Physical Education National Curriculum and inclusion

Introduction

The subject of PE has been at the centre of many changes during the last few years in relation to its recognition, prominence and delivery within the NC. In the primary sector, the introduction of the numeracy and literacy hours in the late 1990s brought about a significant squeeze on the time available for other subject areas. In addition, the implementation of the Key Stage Three strategy and its focus on English, Maths and Science from September 2002, brought with it similar issues and pressures for PE within the secondary sector.

In noting this, however, the NC (2000) does advocate an entitlement of two hours of physical activity within the school week for all children. Furthermore, the Government's PESSCL strategy (2002) has supported the development of physical activity by dedicating £459 million from central government funding. In addition, by 2010 the PE, School Sport and Club Links (PESSCL) strategy aims to offer all children at least four hours of sport every week, comprising of at least two hours of high quality PE and sport at school and the opportunity for at least a further two to three hours beyond the school day (delivered by a range of school, community and club providers). Naturally, children with SEN will have the same entitlement and teachers and schools will need to ensure that their needs are met alongside all other pupils.

This chapter sets out to examine the NC for PE (2000) (QCA 1999a) and its relevance to children with SEN. In addition to examining the six areas of activity, it will look at the principles of the statutory inclusion statement and the expectations that are placed on schools and teachers alike. The subject of PE will be analysed in relation to its structure, organisation and delivery, and potential to link to wider sporting opportunities as part of an examination of 'disability sports' activities.

The chapter concludes by highlighting a range of issues and themes that are emerging related to ensuring that PE teachers are sufficiently equipped to include children with SEN within mainstream settings. As with all the other chapters, and what can be seen as a central theme to this book, this chapter highlights the need for teachers to approach tasks with flexibility, high expectations of children with SEN and a willingness to engage in modification and adaptation as a crucial element in ensuring successful outcomes for the individuals concerned.

Defining and interpreting PE

According to the QCA, PE:

> is the process of developing pupils' knowledge, skills and understanding so that they can perform reflectively and with increasing physical competence and confidence. This process requires pupils to think as well as perform.
>
> (QCA 1999a: 1)

As a result, PE is concerned with involvement and development of physical skills, knowledge of the body in action, and attitudes to engagement in physical activity. Consequently, PE requires children to be predominantly physically active in order to improve skilfulness and develop learning in which growing competence leads to personal confidence, and increased self-esteem.

The purpose of the PE curriculum is to provide:

> the range of tasks, contexts and environments so that an individual's skills can be tuned, adjusted, adapted, modified and refined. The challenge of teaching is to provide information, ideas and encouragement for each pupil to become competent and confident in each new task, context and environment and then extend them again.
>
> (QCA 1999a: 1)

Within this backdrop, the PE curriculum is delivered through six activity areas of dance, games, gymnastics, athletics, outdoor and adventurous activities, and swimming and water safety. This broad, balanced and relevant curriculum seeks to provide children with a diverse range of experiences in order to develop and extend their physical and personal development, as well as their general well-being.

This provision, as part of the NC 2000 (QCA 1999a), should be made available to all children, including those with SEN. As a result, teachers will often need to think in different ways about what and how they are going to teach, whilst making best use of their differentiation, teaching and learning strategies. Sugden and Talbot (1998) support this view, and suggest that teaching children with SEN is merely an extension of teachers' mixed ability teaching. Thus, flexibility of teaching and learning strategy is central to successful inclusive PE. This view is similar to that of Dyson and Millward 2000, Ainscow *et al*. 1999, and Skrtic 1995, which places the emphasis for change on teachers, and stresses the need for them to be pro-active and adapt the curriculum to meet the individual needs of children with SEN.

The NC (2000) divides PE into four areas:

- acquiring and developing skills;
- selecting and applying skills, tactics and compositional ideas;
- knowledge and understanding of fitness and health;
- evaluating and improving performance.

These sections, delivered through the six areas of activity, and with acknowledgement of the principles of the Statutory Inclusion Statement (i.e. setting suitable learning challenges; responding to pupils' diverse learning needs; and overcoming potential barriers to learning and assessment) establish the context for the implementation of the PE curriculum in primary, secondary and special schools.

Task 4.1 The four content areas of PE
Reflect upon the four content areas of the PE NC (2000) and consider what issues you may need to address in order to effectively include children with SEN.

PE NC content area	Issues which need to be considered for children with SEN
Acquiring and developing skills	
Selecting and applying skills, tactics and compositional ideas	
Knowledge and understanding of fitness and health	
Evaluating and improving performance	

The National Curriculum for PE and children with SEN

The revised NC for PE (2000) (QCA 1999a) suggests teachers should consider assessment in alternative activities, with flexible judgements and contexts in order to facilitate access to the curriculum for pupils with SEN. It states, 'teachers must take action' and 'ensure that their pupils are enabled to participate' (QCA 1999a: 33) and be responsive to a diverse range of pupil needs in order to facilitate inclusive education. In meeting this requirement, teachers will need to actively review their pedagogical practices in order to ensure they meet the statutory requirements to facilitate entitlement and accessibility to inclusive activities for all pupils, including those with SEN.

In order to satisfactorily address the needs of pupils with SEN, Farrell suggests teachers must be willing to move beyond an acknowledgment of inclusion policies and be prepared 'to reconsider their structure, teaching approaches, pupil grouping and use of support' (Farrell 1998: 81).

This position supports earlier work noted by Ainscow (1999) who advocates a notion of 'moving schools' that are constantly evolving and changing to be responsive to the needs of the pupils it serves.

The four key principles related to equality, identified in the 1992 NC for PE (DoE 1992), still hold true today as guiding principles when including pupils with SEN within mainstream PE (Vickerman 1997, Vickerman *et al.* 2003). These are **entitlement, accessibility, integration and integrity**, and have acted as the cornerstones upon which the NC for PE (2000) (QCA 1999a) has been revised and extended. In relation to **entitlement**, the premise is to acknowledge the fundamental right of pupils with SEN to access the PE curriculum. This is of particular relevance with the emergence of the SEN and Disability Rights Act (DfES 2001c), which gives pupils a fundamental right to inclusive activity, and the revised *Code of Practice* (DfES 2001b) implemented in January 2002. The *Code of Practice* now focuses much more on the action of schools and teachers to implement and deliver inclusive PE through further delegation of centralised SEN budgets and a requirement to think in different ways about their teaching provision (Dyson 2001, Dyson and Millward 2000, Skrtic 1995).

Teachers are expected therefore to take action within their individual school contexts, and modify and adapt practices in order to facilitate full entitlement to the curriculum for pupils with SEN. This shift in legislation recognises the philosophy of positive attitudes and open minds (Vickerman 2002), and the commitment to a process that offers inclusive education, in which teachers overcome potential barriers through consultation and the adoption of diverse learning, teaching and assessment strategies (Ainscow 1999, Dyson 2001, Dyson and Millward 2000, Sugden and Talbot 1998). This position is to some extent now being reflected in the 02/02 (TTA 2002) Professional Standards Framework (TTA 2002) with the expectation that trainee teachers will demonstrate evidence of differentiated teaching, response to equal opportunities and diversity, and the promotion of positive values.

In terms of **accessibility**, it is the responsibility of teachers to make PE lessons accessible and relevant to the child with SEN. This supports the social model of disability (Reiser and Mason 1990) in which teachers adjust their teaching in order to accommodate the needs of individual pupils rather than the child's disability (medical model) being seen as the barrier to participation. In examining the need to make PE lessons relevant and accessible, it is important to acknowledge the earlier view of Sugden and Talbot (1998), who suggest that teaching pupils with SEN is part of an extension of mixed ability teaching. Teachers should therefore possess many of the skills necessary to facilitate inclusive PE, and consequently may only occasionally require specialist advice and guidance.

Thus, the fundamental factor in a successful inclusive activity for pupils with SEN is a positive attitude, suitable differentiation and a readiness to modify existing practice within PE lessons (Farrell 1998). Whilst there may be a few difficulties for teachers to embrace more inclusive approaches, the PE profession is well placed to embrace inclusive practice, and to a large extent the process has begun with the increased focus on aspects of inclusion within PE, education and society in general (Fredrickson and Cline 2002, Dyson 2001, Vickerman *et al.* 2003).

However, the critical success factors in the drive to more inclusive PE will be the training and support given to trainee teachers, newly qualified teachers and schools within process models which reflect implementation of 'policy through to practice' (Depauw and Doll-Tepper 2000, Westwood 1997). As a result, ITT providers, schools and statutory agencies need to ensure that future teachers are adequately prepared to deliver this inclusive agenda. Consequently, as part of the drive to a more co-ordinated approach, the DfES *Schools Achieving Success* (DfES 2001a) publication advocates greater levels of multi-agency and collaborative working practices in the years ahead.

The third principle of **integration** recognises the benefits of disabled and non-disabled pupils being educated together and the positive outcomes, which can be achieved for all pupils through such approaches. Whilst concepts of integration have moved on since 1992 (now embracing concepts of inclusion), these can be seen as fundamental stepping-stones towards inclusive practice (Slininger *et al.* 2000), ultimately recognising difference but treating pupils appropriately and according to their learning needs. This also begins to address the UK Government's citizenship agenda in which pupils are to be educated to have mutual understanding and respect for individual diversity as part of their involvement and participation within a socially inclusive society. PE is an ideal vehicle for this to occur, with many activities involving teamwork and co-operation.

PE teachers need to underpin their learning and teaching practice with **integrity,** and a recognition that they value and believe in the adaptations and changes that are made to the activities they teach. As part of this personal commitment, they should ensure that inclusive PE for pupils with SEN is of equal worth, challenging, and in no way patronising or demeaning to the individual child concerned. PE teachers should therefore adopt approaches which set appropriate and challenging tasks (NC 2000 Statutory Inclusion Statement (QCA 1999a)) to pupils who have additional learning needs whilst avoiding the 'cotton wool' approach, which often assumes that these pupils cannot cope with some of the demands that a challenging curriculum may offer (Goodwin and Watkinson 2000, Sherrill 1998, Vickerman *et al.* 2003). Consequently, this may involve schools and teachers re-examining their present teaching philosophies, attitudes, values and cultures with the intention of establishing flexible yet challenging educational experiences for children with SEN (Centre for Studies in Inclusive Education 2000).

Task 4.2 Principles of equality of opportunity
Reflect on the four principles of entitlement, accessibility, integration and integrity and develop your understanding of each of these, then look at what you will need to do to ensure children with SEN gain positive experiences in their PE lessons.

Principles of equality of opportunity in PE	Your interpretation of the principle	Action you need to take to ensure children gain positive outcomes
Entitlement		
Accessibility		
Integration		
Integrity		

Adapted PE and sport

In conjunction with definitions, interpretations and contexts related to the PE curriculum in the UK, extensive work has been undertaken in the development of 'adapted PE', 'adapted sport' and 'disability sport' both in the UK and in the USA. These strategies support and extend provision within the formal school curriculum, and have to a certain extent shaped the delivery of present day PE and school sport for children with SEN. Winnick (2000) suggests that 'Adapted physical education is a sub-discipline of physical education that allows for safe, personally satisfying and successful participation to meet the unique needs of students' (Winnick 2000: 4).

Adapted PE is designed to meet the long-term (i.e. over 30 days) unique needs of disabled children, and establish common frameworks for their inclusion within PE programmes (Auxter *et al.* 2001, Winnick 2000). As Winnick says, 'Adapted physical education is an individualised program of physical and motor fitness; fundamental motor skills and patterns; and skills . . . designed to meet the unique needs of individuals' (Winnick 2000: 4).

In contrast:

> Adapted sport refers to sport modified or created to meet the unique needs of individuals with disabilities. Adapted sport may be conducted in integrated settings in which individuals with disabilities interact with non-disabled participants or in segregated environments that only include those persons with disabilities.
>
> (Winnick 2000: 5)

The use of the term 'adapted sport' is preferred to 'disability sport' as it stimulates and encourages participation and excellence in a variety of settings, rather than categorising activity that specifically caters for disabled people alone (Auxter *et al.* 2001, Depauw and Gavron 1995, Winnick 2000). This supports the recent shift towards inclusive activity in which children with SEN participate within the same inclusive environment as their non-disabled peers. To some extent this shift is also being seen within national and international disability sport – for example, adults in the Sydney 2000 Olympics and the Manchester 2002 Commonwealth Games competed at the same venue and at the same time.

Auxter *et al.* (2001) argues within the contexts of adapted PE and sport that it is crucial for teachers to assume responsibility for all children and adults that they work with, regardless of individual needs. Winnick supports this view in suggesting:

> A good teacher and/or coach of children places the development of positive self esteem as a priority and displays an attitude of acceptance, empathy, friendship and warmth, while ensuring a secure and controlled environment. The good teacher or coach of adapted physical education and sport selects and uses teaching approaches and styles beneficial to students, provides individualised and personalised instruction and opportunities, and creates a positive environment where students can succeed.
>
> (Winnick 2000: 8)

This supports the current evolving thinking on the practice, structure and delivery of inclusion within the UK in which flexibility, adaptation and openness to change are seen as critical success factors (Dyson and Millward 2000, Ainscow 1999, Skrtic 1991, 1995).

Evolving practice in inclusive PE and sport

Whilst the most significant progress in adapted activity has recently focused on educational services for disabled children and adults, the use of physical activity as part of exercise and therapy for treatment is not a new concept, and dates back to as early as 3000 BC in China. The Romans and Greeks also recognised the benefits of therapy and the value of exercise as a means of assisting with mobility and general health and well-being (Winnick 2000, Auxter *et al.* 2001). Developments in physical activity and remedial therapy date back many years and have contributed to arriving at more con-temporary approaches to inclusive PE and sport for children with SEN. Sherill (1998) notes that the 1800s and early part of the 1900s, for example, were initially characterised by medical orientation of therapy, prevention, rehabil-itation and cure.

However, there was a shift from the 1930s to the modern day, and now thinking has shifted from the medical to the 'whole person' approach, which runs in tandem with educational developments moving from segre-gated to inclusive, person-centred strategies. Within the context of 'whole person orientations', Winnick (2000) suggests individuals who require physical activity programmes as part of their disability should be assessed according to their particular needs, then programmes should be established that best fit their particular needs. This is in line with modern day concepts of inclusive practice within schools, in which teachers and schools change and adapt their provision to meet the individual needs of children with SEN, rather than the other way around (Ainscow 1999).

In shifting to more inclusive practices, Winnick established a framework of 'alternative instructional placements' within the PE curriculum that were based on strategies moving from conventional medical models of treatment and separate centres which he described as 'most restrictive', through to 'regular' inclusive placements which were 'least restrictive' in terms of devel-oping the child with SEN as a whole. 'Least restrictive environments' accord-ing to Winnick (2000) need teachers to focus upon the curriculum, teaching styles and organisational strategies. In facilitating an inclusive (least restric-tive) curriculum, for example, lessons should be based on developmentally appropriate activities, centred according to Winnick upon 'Craft's (1996) four curricula options', namely:

- **same curriculum** – access to the same activity areas within the curriculum;
- **multi-level curriculum** – pursuing different objectives, but within the same lesson;
- **curriculum overlap** – involving modification of the curriculum;
- **alternative curriculum** – separate or disability specific activities.

Thus, there is an expectation that teachers adopt a range of flexible teaching, learning and organisational approaches to deliver inclusive PE for children with SEN (Farrell 1998, Sugden and Talbot 1998, QCA 1999a). Craft's (1996) 'curricula options' complement recent thinking in the development of the 'inclusion spectrum', which builds upon Winnick's notion of flexible teaching and learning strategies and has been extended by the Youth Sport Trust and the EFDS. The inclusion spectrum offers a range of strategies that teachers can move in and out of during their lessons in order to ensure maximum participation and access to physical activity for children with SEN. These strategies are, however, not solely related to including children with SEN and can, as many authors have suggested (Wright and Sugden 1999, Farrell 1998), be used to create greater flexibility in teaching and learning to include all pupils. The inclusion spectrum suggests five strategies of open, modified, parallel, separate, and disability sport activities that enable teachers to deliver PE in conjunction with the principles of the NC (2000) Statutory Inclusion Statement (QCA 1999a) (see Figure 4.1).

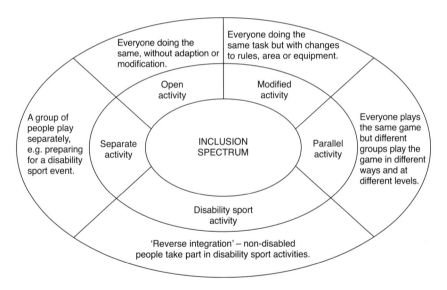

Figure 4.1 The inclusion spectrum.
Source: Youth Sport Trust

Task 4.3 The range of teaching and learning strategies
Reflect upon the range of teaching and learning strategies discussed to date in this chapter and consider which you feel will fit best with the pupils you teach and your personal teaching philosophies and ideologies.

Extending and developing teaching and learning strategies in PE

As part of their general teaching philosophy and practices, teachers should seek to embrace the guiding principles of entitlement, accessibility, integration and integrity. This should be undertaken alongside contemporary notions of inclusion and flexible teaching and learning strategies if teachers are to make a genuine commitment to inclusive PE for pupils with SEN. Additionally, as part of the revised NC for PE (2000) (QCA 1999a), teachers need to spend time interpreting the Inclusion Statement, whilst recognising the need to set suitable learning challenges, respond to pupils' diverse needs and overcome potential barriers to learning and assessment for individuals and groups of pupils. The strategies and models offered in the 'four curricula options' (Craft 1996), 'inclusion spectrum' and 'continuum of alternative instructional placements in physical education' (Winnick 2000) are valuable starting points for teachers to consider their approach to inclusive PE.

In relation to 'setting suitable learning challenges', the NC for PE (2000) (QCA 1999a) states that 'Teachers should aim to give every pupil the opportunity to experience success in learning and to achieve as high a standard as is possible' (QCA 1999a: 28). It suggests this can be achieved by teaching knowledge, skills and understanding of PE from earlier key stages, if appropriate, with the aim of ensuring those pupils with SEN progress and achieve. It could be argued, therefore, that inclusion for pupils with SEN is about focusing upon earlier developmental expectations, or adopting a more flexible teaching approach to accommodate individuals' needs in terms of learning, teaching and assessment. Sugden and Talbot (1998), for example, support this view through the principles of 'moving to learn' and 'learning to move'. They argue: 'Physical education has a distinctive role to play, because it is not simply about education of the physical but involves cognitive, social, language and moral development and responsibilities' (Sugden and Talbot 1998: 22). Thus, to facilitate inclusion, a shift away from the traditional (learning to move) outcome of PE in which skills are taught and learned, to a wider experience of PE (moving to learn) may be one such approach in enabling access to inclusive PE.

PE teachers need to consider their learning outcomes carefully in order to ensure all pupils with SEN have the opportunity to demonstrate a wide variety of movement learning experiences, and this links with the principle of 'responding to pupils' diverse learning needs'. Consequently, the NC for PE (2000) states: 'when planning teachers should set high expectations and provide opportunities for all pupils to achieve including . . . pupils with disabilities and special educational needs' (QCA 1999a: 29).

This section suggests lessons should be planned to ensure full and effective access, and that teachers need to be aware of equal opportunity legislation.

This begins to answer some of Dyson's (1999) concerns that the curriculum needs to focus on how outcomes can be differentiated and measured for each child, rather than focusing upon philosophical definitions of equality. A key feature is that this will need to be based upon the social model of disability and a commitment to change the activity to fit the child rather than the other way around (Vickerman 1997).

In terms of 'overcoming potential barriers to learning and assessment for individuals and groups of pupils' the NC for PE (2000) states that 'a minority of pupils will have particular learning and assessment requirements which go beyond the provisions described earlier (sections one and two) and if not addressed could create barriers to participation' (QCA 1999a: 30). The document indicates this is usually as a consequence of a child's disability or SEN. The curriculum suggests that in creating access, greater differentiation on the part of teachers and the use of external agencies or specialist equipment will begin to enable inclusion to occur. This statement is fundamental in ensuring that teachers recognise their full responsibility for creating accessible lessons that cater for all pupils' needs, whilst recognising the need to work through a multi-agency approach to deliver inclusive activities (Depauw and Doll-Tepper 2000). This means teachers will need to have different expectations of some pupils with SEN, and/or will need to modify assessment in ways that offer children the opportunity to demonstrate development of their knowledge and understanding.

The strategies outlined so far aim to move in the direction of 'least restrictive' activities within a context of support within 'regular', inclusive environments. This changing teaching philosophy reflects many of the legislative changes that have occurred over recent years to support this practice (SEN and Disability Right Act, DfES 2001c, Code of Practice, DfES 2001b, QCA 1999a). Within this backdrop the modern day approach to physical activity for disabled adults and children with SEN is to work towards an integration continuum for sport participation that supports regular (inclusive), rather than segregated (restrictive), provision (Winnick 1987). The model indicated in the earlier work of Winnick (1987) succinctly emphasises the context within which inclusive education for children with SEN should be established in the future.

In reviewing the diverse range of teaching and learning models designed for the inclusion of children with SEN in PE it could be argued that they can be grouped into three categories (Block and Volger 1994, Giangreco *et al*. 1993). These are based around:

- **curriculum adaptation** – changing what is taught;
- **instructional modifications** – changing how we teach;
- **human or people resources** – looking at changing who teaches or supports adapted aspects of PE.

These models have led to the successful inclusion of many children with SEN (Volger and Romance 2000, Slinger *et al.* 2000, Goodwin and Watkinson 2000). As a result, statutory agencies, teacher training providers, schools, trainee teachers and practitioners should structure their future training and development around these three factors in order to progress inclusion for children with SEN.

Many of the studies undertaken into good practice identify critical success factors related to teaching and learning, yet are patchier in gauging the views and opinions of children with SEN related to their experiences of inclusive PE (Dyson and Millward 2000, Ainscow 1999, Skrtic 1991, 1995, Volger and Romance 2000, Slininger *et al.* 2000). However, Goodwin and Watkinson (2000) identified a distinction between what they refer to as 'good days and bad days' for children with SEN in inclusive PE. The study found children with SEN who were involved in positive, inclusive PE experiences described the 'good days' as being engaged in learning contexts with modified practices to accommodate their needs, feelings of progression in skill development, sense of belonging, and the support of teachers who were prepared to adopt flexible approaches to their involvement. These experiences support many of the issues noted earlier based upon curriculum adaptation, instructional modifications and human resources. In contrast, 'bad days' involved restricted participation (Winnick 2000) in which, due to a lack of flexibility of approach, children with SEN felt isolated, demotivated, lacking in self-esteem and engaged in learning environments where teachers had not planned effectively for their involvement.

In support of these findings, Place and Hodge (2001) looked at the behaviour of disabled and non-disabled children when engaged in inclusive PE related to levels of social interaction between the two groups of children. They found inclusive PE can lead to increased social interaction, but only if there is full recognition and due regard for inclusive PE as a process, which is practised within a context of:

- **appropriate curricula adaptations** – recognising and valuing diversity, and planning effectively for its implementation;
- **instructional modifications** – based upon sound pedagogical practices that enhance rather than restrict inclusive activity;
- **sound human resources** – incorporating PE teachers who are well equipped to deliver inclusive PE;
- **informed decision-making** – based on consultation, reflection, and a readiness to modify and adapt strategies to facilitate inclusive activity.

Slininger *et al.* (2000) support this view in their advocacy of 'contact theory' in which they argue that, in order to eliminate prejudice and discrimination, and establish environments that are conducive to learning, teachers must plan effectively for inclusive lessons. They found that if teachers did not plan inclusive lessons, many shared opportunities for learning and development were missed and the overall success of inclusive learning was limited. This research demonstrates the need for teachers to spend time planning effectively for inclusion within a context of readiness to change, and modify existing teaching and learning strategies.

Practical examples of inclusive PE for children with SEN

When planning inclusive PE for pupils with SEN it is important to start from the premise of full inclusion, and, where this may not be possible, to consider adaptation or modification of learning and teaching activities (Winnick 1987, 2000). A central success factor for teachers is to consult, where appropriate, with the child with SEN and relevant professionals as part of a multi-disciplinary approach. This enables the pupil and teachers to consider, at the planning stage, any differentiation that may be required (Goodwin and Watkinson 2000). This supports principles of equality and the social model approach, which acknowledges individual diversity whilst also responding to the needs of pupils with SEN by modifying or adapting activities as appropriate (NC 2000 Statutory Inclusion Statement, QCA 1999a).

An example of this could be in games activities such as hockey, where pupils may initially require lighter, larger or different coloured balls in order to access the activity. Adaptations to rules may need to be considered, such as allowing a player with movement restrictions five seconds to receive and play the ball. If utilising such a strategy, it is vital that all members of the group understand the need for such an adaptation (Slinger and Sherrill 2000) in order that they can play to this rule during a game. In dance, activities can be adapted through consultation with the disabled and non-disabled pupils, as part of the requirements of the curriculum to work co-operatively. A pupil in a wheelchair, for example, can use the chair as an extension of their body to move around a particular area. If group tasks are to be performed, then the group can work together on themes for inclusion in which the movement patterns of the pupils with SEN can be incorporated into the overall group piece being performed (Vickerman *et al.* 2003).

Another example of inclusive participation in athletic activities with physically disabled pupils may involve one push of their wheelchair, rather than a jump into the sandpit, or reducing distances to run or travel. If there are pupils with visual impairments teachers can organise activities such as a 100-metre race in which a guide stands at the finish line and shouts out the lane number they are in, or a guide runs alongside them for support. Many of the suggestions indicated above support the points noted earlier of needing to be open to change whilst recognising that this work is as an integral component of a PE teacher's general mixed ability teaching (Sugden and Talbot 1998). Consequently, the attitude of mind and motivation to change existing teaching and learning practices is central to successful inclusive activity (Dyson and Millward 2000, Ainscow 1999, Farrell 1998).

Concluding thoughts and a rationale for inclusive PE

The NC for PE (2000) clearly supports the notion of inclusion through a set of statements that are based upon ensuring that teachers set suitable learning challenges; respond to pupils' diverse learning needs; and overcome potential barriers to learning and assessment in order to accommodate all children's needs. However, in setting out to achieve such an inclusive approach, Dyson (1999) notes some concern with the concept of disability now being 'at the heart of a new and privileged society' (Dyson 1999: 2).

According to Dyson, 'social inclusion' is limited as it only pursues measures to remove difference that focus upon predicted equality, and are not necessarily outcome based. Therefore implementation of policies by government agencies and schools may appear to be socially and morally right, but the danger is that measurement will be through expectations for statements written into policies. However, success should be judged in terms of its impact and effects upon a child's quality of education and achievement. (See Depauw and Doll-Tepper 2000, Dyson 2001, Farrell 2000, 2001 for further issues related to policy implementation and practice.) Thus, greater focus in the future must be turned to the development of facilitating inclusive practice through pedagogical practices, rather than simply making policy statements of intent (Dyson 1999, 2001, Dyson and Millward 2000).

On examining the inclusion statement in relation to PE, these fundamental requirements, in conjunction with recent legislative changes, will require PE teachers to ensure they are fulfilling all their statutory and professional practice responsibilities. As a consequence, teachers need to ensure they facilitate and empower children with SEN to have full entitlement and accessibility to the curriculum. The PE Handbook, which accompanies the revised NC, sets an expectation that the curriculum should be based around the key principle of openness and accessibility and a belief that 'equality of opportunity is one of a broad set of common values and purposes which underpin the school curriculum and the work of schools' (QCA 1999b: 4).

Dyson (1999) supports such a move as part of the process model that moves beyond recognition of principles and philosophical standpoints and into the practice of action based upon how the curriculum relates to outcomes that can be differentiated and measured for each child. A key feature of this occurring will need to be based upon a strong emphasis of consultation between teachers, pupils with SEN, parents and professionals (Vickerman 1997, 2002). This will need to be undertaken within the context of models of best practice in teaching and learning in inclusive education noted earlier (Dyson 2001, Farrell 1998, Winnick 2000, Goodwin and Watkinson 2000).

Task 4.4 Process models of inclusive practice

Reflect upon Dyson's (1999) view of inclusion for children with SEN in PE needing to be part of a process model that moves from philosophy to action based practice. Use the table below to review your understanding of the process model and what strategies you may employ in PE to ensure successful experiences for children with SEN.

Key aspects to consider in moving from philosophy to action	Review your understanding of the terms	Action required as part of your teaching and learning strategies
What are key principles?		
What are philosophical standpoints?		
What is action based practice?		
What is a curriculum that relates to outcomes differentiated for each child?		
What are strategies for consultation?		

The PE handbooks (QCA 1999a, 1999b) indicate that a minority of pupils will have particular learning and assessment requirements which go beyond the provisions described earlier and, if not addressed, could create barriers to participation, and this is usually as a consequence of a child's' disability or SEN. In suggesting methods to overcome potential barriers to participation, the handbook states that in order to create access, greater differentiation on the part of teachers and the use of external agencies or specialist equipment will begin to enable inclusion to occur. This statement is fundamental in ensuring that teachers recognise their responsibility in creating accessible lessons that cater for all pupils' needs.

Westwood (1997) supports the promotion of citizenship and the social model of disability within the curriculum, as a means of shifting the emphasis away from the pupils with the disability to the roles that teachers and non-disabled peers can play in facilitating all children's learning. However, Westwood notes some caution in ignoring the complexity of defining inclusion and its current ability to be interpreted by teachers, due to their lack of clarity and training in this subject. If, as the NC for PE (2000) suggests, 'Teachers must take action' and 'Ensure that their pupils are enabled to participate' (QCA 1999a: 33), a greater focus on the consideration of models of best practice in teaching and learning pedagogy will need to be considered and shared by all teachers within the profession. However, you as an individual can make a difference to children with SEN and you should remember to both stimulate discussion with colleagues whilst ensuring your practice meets the needs of the children concerned.

Chapter 5

Planning for and assessing children with special educational needs

Introduction

This chapter sets out to review the strategies that are necessary for planning for and assessing children with SEN in PE. In any PE lesson the importance of setting suitable learning challenges through clear expectations, knowledge of individual children, flexibility, and a commitment to modification and adaptive practices is essential. As a result, if we plan our teaching and objectives around these central principles we should employ the same strategies in relation to assessing children with SEN knowledge and understanding. The chapter will help you to review your understanding of what, why and how we assess children in PE, whilst assisting you to consider diverse strategies to ensure individuals have the best chance to demonstrate competence in PE.

Assessment should be considered as a process, which gives both the child with SEN and the teacher an insight into learning which is associated with a permanent change in the behaviour of the learner. In order to ascertain whether learning in PE has taken place, it must be assessed to see if the learning outcomes have been achieved. It is through this process that teachers provide a constructive foundation for future planning and target setting of pupils with SEN. Furthermore, assessment provides a valuable activity for teachers in judging their own teaching, learning and planning, and highlighting effective and ineffective aspects of this process. Thus assessment can act as a dual strategy both to assist the pupil with SEN and to enable the teacher to quantify their own learning and development.

A central tenet of this dual assessment process is the need for teachers to be aware of the second and third aspects of the PE NC Statutory Inclusion Statement. These require teachers to respond to pupils' diverse needs (thus requiring flexibility in assessment design) and to overcome potential barriers to learning and assessment for individuals and groups of pupils. As a result, teachers deliver this by getting to know the individual needs of children and ensuring that assessment strategies are established to help children with SEN demonstrate knowledge and understanding of PE through flexible approaches rather than being highly prescriptive about the specific method to be utilised.

When should assessment take place for children with SEN?

Assessment is critical to the learning of new skills and understanding how this information can be utilised to progress learning for children with SEN. It is important, therefore, to ensure that every child, regardless of their ability and range of SEN, is working to their full potential. This will require teachers to have a good knowledge of the individual needs of children and a commitment to be adaptable and have high expectations of what children with SEN can achieve. As movement is a central component of PE and is very often assessed, many of the examples in this chapter will be drawn from this setting in order to exemplify your understanding of the process.

According to Capel (2001), assessment 'covers all the activities undertaken by teachers and others to measure the effectiveness of teaching and learning (Capel 2001: 287). Consequently, assessment in PE takes place for many reasons, for example in selecting or grouping pupils, as an indicator of how well a task or concept is understood, to motivate pupils, monitor progress, or more generally to give feedback to teacher, pupil and parents. However, an important issue to consider as part of any assessment strategy is to ask the question, for what purposes do we need to collect, analyse, store and retrieve data? Thus it is important, as it helps to determine how information will be meaningful to the pupil, teacher and parent rather than just fulfilling the school assessment policy. This view is supported by Frapwell et al. (2000), who state, 'To view assessment as divorced from the planning, teaching and learning process results in the implementation of a meaningless bolt on model, a bureaucratic monster or a task to satisfy senior management requirements' (Frapwell 2002: 24).

If assessment is to play an important role in the teaching and learning process it should not be seen as purely a 'bolt on' process; in contrast, it needs to be seen as an activity that has the potential to occur all the time in the PE lesson. This is known as 'formative assessment', which means it is ongoing throughout their lesson and helps both you as the teacher and the child gain insight into how they are doing at any particular point in the lesson. Formative feedback is a vital aspect of any assessment process as it offers ongoing, current and context led feedback at a time when the child understands and appreciates it. For children with SEN, formative feedback is especially important because teachers needs to identify a pupil's movement concepts and motor skills, what the body does in specific contexts, where the body moves, how the body moves and with whom or with what the body moves. It is vital that these basic movement patterns are established

---

Task 5.1 Why and how we assess

Use the table below to review your thoughts on why we assess and how we use the data to help our understanding of the needs of children with SEN in PE.

Aspects of assessment	Your understanding of the issues
Why do we assess?	
For what purposes do we need to collect information?	
What do you understand by responding to pupils' diverse needs in assessment?	
How can you overcome potential barriers to learning and assessment for individuals and groups of pupils?	
How and why do we analyse information on children with SEN?	
How and why do we store assessment data?	
For what purposes should we retrieve and report assessment data?	

for children with poor motor skills, in order to move onto more specialist skills. Thus, a child might have good control when using small movements, but large motor movements, such as catching or kicking a ball, may prove more difficult. The assessment strategy needs to identify these children and their specific needs in order to minimise frustration and so that negativity and fear of failure do not set in on the part of the individual concerned.

What is it that we should be assessing in PE?

Developing and supporting children's movement patterns is a critical part of PE and wider life and social skills, which include activities such as walking, jogging, sprinting, throwing and catching a ball, and jumping. These movement patterns can be described through the analysis and description of definitive arrangements of muscle actions, which are required to fulfil the desired outcomes in any lesson. However, assessment is not just about observing movement patterns and motor skills, rather it can be described as an integrated process that builds up a picture of the whole child.

A significant amount of work on movement has been influenced by Laban's framework (see Laban 1942) and this considers movement to be not only of prime importance in the shaping of attitudes and relationships but also a vital force in education. Bailey (1999) supports this view by suggesting that 'there is little doubting the central importance of movement and physical activity in the lives of children and young people'. In his research he found physical play was the first appearing and most frequently occurring expression in infants and physical competence as a second and major factor that influences social acceptance in children of all ages and both sexes. Thus, there is a need to build a picture of the strengths and weaknesses of children with SEN; not just in relation to motor skills but how this affects the child emotionally and whether self-concept, self-esteem and motivation levels are impacted upon as well. Consequently, when teachers work with children with SEN they should be asking questions such as:

- Is a lack of motor skills affecting other areas of learning?
- Does a lack of motor skills affect the child's interaction with others?
- Are children with SEN generally unhappy with their general physical competence?
- Is there other behaviour occurring as a result of the child's difficulty with movement?
- If movement is seen to be enjoyable and meaningful, how does this impact on children's everyday life skills and experiences and are they more likely to achieve success in PE?

In reviewing the questions above with an open mind and commitment to flexible teaching, learning and assessment strategies you will be able to plan for effective inclusion whilst identifying any potential barriers to participation, and then be in a position to take action as required. With regard to assessing children with SEN at the end of PE lessons this supports pupils' learning, motivates pupils through feedback and progress to date and provides a context for the next lesson. This type of **formative** assessment will help the teacher identify poor motor ability, which can have a serious effect on behaviour and motivation in all areas of the curriculum. If a child with SEN (as with their non-disabled peers) continually experiences failure, frustration will set in, which in turn will lead to individuals becoming demotivated, and they will begin to get into a negative spiral about experiences and participation in PE.

Teachers should also assess at the end of a series of lessons as this helps with the monitoring of pupils' progress and achievement and provides feedback to individuals to help them consolidate their skills over a period of time. This can also be an opportunity for the teacher to give positive feedback to the child about areas of permanent addition to the learning skills and abilities of the individual concerned. Finally assessment at the end of a year helps in the reviewing of pupils' strengths and identifies areas for development, focuses on activity and personal development, and forms the basis for a report to the pupils and parents about the progress they have made in all aspects of the years work.

In the NC for PE (2000) attainment targets are used in the assessment of pupils, and they set out the knowledge, skills and understanding that pupils of different abilities and maturities are expected to have at particular ages. They consist of eight level descriptions of increasing difficulty, with each level descriptor identifying the types and range of performance that pupils working at that level should characteristically demonstrate. For example, the NC grade descriptors for levels one and two set out below use level descriptors where teachers need to judge which description best fits the pupil's performance in PE. This is where your ability to approach assessment judgements flexibly and use the descriptors as a guide for interpretation in relation to individual children with SEN is critical.

At level 1 pupils copy, repeat and explore simple skills and actions requiring basic control and co-ordination. They start to link these skills and actions in ways which suit the activities. They describe and comment on their own and others' actions. They talk about how to exercise safely, and how their bodies feel during an activity.

At level 2 pupils explore simple skills. They copy, remember, repeat and explore simple actions with control and co-ordination. They vary skills, actions and ideas and link these in ways that suit the activities. They begin to show some understanding of simple tactics and basic compositional ideas. They talk about differences between their own and others' performance and suggest improvements. They understand how to exercise safely, and describe how their bodies feel during different activities.

In order to use these level descriptors, teachers need to adopt flexible assessment strategies to be able to ensure they meet the needs of specific pupils. An example of this could be shown by linking the statements in with the movement ABC (see Henderson and Sugden 1992 and page 76 of this chapter). This offers a far more rounded picture of the level the child was working at. The levels include the children describing and commentating on their own work and that of others, which gives the child more 'ownership' of the task. This may also identify the child who actually understands the movement but is not controlled when carrying out the task. At level 1, copying, repeating and exploring simple actions can include things like posture and using simple games to explore changes of speed and direction to improve control and consistency. These games can also include jumping, hopping and skipping activities which will involve various degrees of balance and transfer of weight. These types of movement underpin much more complex tasks, so by including them in a fun way and showing that the tasks have a purpose they are much more likely to be successful.

If throwing tasks are being practised, using targets of different sizes and different distances is far more enjoyable than throwing at a wall or simply just throwing and catching (sending and receiving). Varying the tasks whilst concentrating on the same skill will stop the child becoming bored and help the teacher to form an overall picture of the level the children are working at and the child's individual needs. Getting the children to describe how their bodies feel during exercise is also helping them to understand what happens to their bodies during physical activity. These actions fit into the visual, audio and kinaesthetic model of learning, and should encourage children to observe themselves and others, listen to feedback, give feedback on their observations, and describe how their bodies feel during the tasks. This enables them to focus and concentrate more on each individual action and is a critical element in encouraging children with SEN to develop confidently and securely in PE.

The movement ABC

The movement ABC (Henderson and Sugden 1992) is a battery of tests with planned interactions that make the tests more meaningful. The checklist is a screening instrument (for use by teachers) as well as a means for planning intervention. The motor part of the checklist is divided into four sections (12 items in each section) and represents the interaction between the child and the environment. Scores for each item are marked on an ordinal scale 0 to 3 and a total score is calculated, with higher scores indicating higher levels of impairment. Factor analysis indicated that there were seven factors involved:

1 ball skills (by far the most important, accounting for 49.6 per cent of the variance);
2 static balance, manipulation of fine objects and keeping rhythm;
3 dynamic balance;
4 fine manipulation;
5 avoiding objects or persons;
6 knowledge of body scheme and directional awareness (including vehicle riding);
7 self-care skills.

The implications of this seem to resist the use of a single category for children who have perceptual motor problems and to look rather for relatively specific training, based on meaningful targets in real contexts, and which will be useful to children (either in terms of their educational skills or independence).

This has been supported by a recent intervention study by Chambers and Sugden (2003), where the emphasis was on children performing functional tasks in settings that were as near as possible to everyday life.

However, more qualitative methods are needed to gain the full picture, with a move away from assessment at the end of a unit of work to an understanding that assessment can inform and improve performance throughout the unit. Thus, teachers need more than good assessment instruments, they also need help with methods to interpret and respond to the results in a formative way. The structure of tests therefore needs to reveal the methods used by those tested, to provide teachers with the feedback to best help their pupils.

When applying formative assessments to provide positive results there needs to be a culture of success, which should be backed by a belief that everyone can achieve. Formative assessment 'provides information which can aid further progress, diagnose reasons for both good and poor performance, and target particular learning needs' (Capel 2001: 289). For assessment to be formative, the feedback information has to be used (i.e. feedback has to be meaningful and realistic). If a child with poor motor development is left alone they will develop slowly and not be able to use skills required for daily life. If the child is presented with situations which help them learn in both an intentional and incidental manner then the child learns new skills, which will have a positive influence on his development. In school the so-called 'clumsy child' can stand out from the rest. Early experiences of failure can result in a child having little confidence in learning new skills.

An essential skill needed by teachers to formatively assess pupils is that of observation. Through observation teachers can adjust the tasks in order to match the needs of the individuals. However, Peach and Bamforth highlighted that 'poor observational skills such as carelessness and lack of attention to detail and not applying selective attention may cause the task to be adjusted to the incorrect ability of the child' (Peach and Bamforth 2002: 52). Good observation is dependent on having clear criteria arising from learning objectives. Observing well is dependent on having a number of skills that need to be practised.

How can we assess movement?

There are many ways of assessing movement. The NC level descriptors above should be used alongside the movement ABC and with reference to the *Special Educational Needs Code of Practice* (DfES 2001b). The more information that can be gathered, the easier it is to set specific targets which can form the basis of an individual education plan (IEP) which identifies a child's immediate learning needs by assessing a pupil's progress against these targets. This again needs to be a continuous process to ensure progression and indicate what future action might need to be taken. In relation to the *Special Educational Needs Code of Practice* (DfES 2001b) there are four levels (School Action, School Action Plus, Formal Assessment, Statement of SEN) which teachers need to be aware of when making judgements about the nature and level of support required by pupils.

School Action

When a member of staff identifies a pupil with SEN, the subject teachers in consultation with the special educational needs co-ordinator (SENCO) devise interventions additional to or different from those provided as part of the school's usual differentiated curriculum. Subject and pastoral teachers still remain responsible for working with the pupil on a daily basis and delivering an individualised programme, usually based around an individual education plan.

School Action Plus

At this stage the SENCO will consult with subject, pastoral staff, parents and the pupil and will ask for help from relevant external agencies. The outside specialists will provide advice and/or support to teachers and the SENCO will action additional or different strategies to those at School Action level, and put in place a new IEP as necessary. Furthermore, the SENCO takes the lead in any further assessment of the pupil, planning future interventions for the child and holding discussions with colleagues as well as monitoring and reviewing action taken.

Formal Assessment (stage three) and Statement of SEN (stage four)

Following a statutory assessment co-ordinated by the local education authority (LEA) a Statement of SEN may be issued. This will detail the pupil's area of need, objectives of the statement and provision to be made to the school. The LEA now takes the lead in any further assessment of the pupil and planning future interventions for the child in discussion with the SENCO and parents via an annual review meeting and/or transition meeting. It is important to note here that schools are under legal obligations to, as far as possible, meet the requirements and recommendations stated in the Statement of SEN.

This formalised assessment of a child's specific needs also meets the Government's *Every Child Matters* agenda (DfES 2005), which sets out to ensure that each and every child has the opportunity to learn and develop according to their particular circumstances. This agenda focuses upon five aspects of ensuring that children are afforded opportunities to:

B: be healthy
E: economic well-being
A: achieve and enjoy
M: make a positive contribution
S: stay safe

The level descriptors, *Every Child Matters* agenda, and the *Code of Practice* are methods of looking at the whole child and how they respond to various situations, and not just their motor abilities. It is therefore looking at the process of how the child performs over time and not just at the end result. This again helps in building up the picture of the child with SEN, reviewing how it makes the child feel when they are successful and listening to comments on how well they performed.

Task 5.2 The four stages of the *Code of Practice*
Using the table below, review the four stages of the *Code of Practice* in conjunction with the five aspects of the *Every Child Matters* agenda. First reflect on your understanding of the terms and stages, then second explore how you can ensure these needs are met as part of your teaching, learning and assessment strategies.

Aspects of the Code of Practice and the Every Child Matters agenda	What is your understanding of these aspects?	How can you ensure they are delivered?
School Action		
School Action Plus		
Formal Assessment		
Statement of SEN		
Being healthy		
Economic well-being		
Achieving and enjoying		
Making a positive contribution		
Staying safe		

Human movement and children with SEN

Human movement has many dimensions; all children want to exploit the body's capacity for movement, and they thrive in any accomplishments they make. A young child uses movement as a means of learning about themselves and the physical world and, however trivial it might seem, to seek recognition and confirmation in an adult's eyes as well as to enjoy movement for its own sake. They experiment, apply and develop movement in many different ways and this provides a two-way channel of learning, both to find out about physical learning and to gain feedback on their particular accomplishments. Indeed, movement should not only be associated with, or isolated within, PE – it happens in a multitude of everyday situations.

A movement pattern is a definite arrangement of muscle actions required to achieve a desired outcome, for example, walking, throwing a ball or jumping in the air. The spatial and rhythmic components remain relatively constant and can be practised, and are essential to achieving the desired outcome. A movement pattern may be likened to a general template, which then becomes a basis for a number of specific skills. This transfer of skills is critical if learning is to take place. To be versatile in movement, children with SEN need the widest possible range of experiences with opportunities for frequent application and practice.

In order to ensure that any human movement is assessed fairly and consistently it is important for teachers to be accurate in any judgements they make (see Bailey 2001). Consequently, when assessing pupils with SEN in PE you need to ensure that your processes are valid, reliable, objective and practical.

Validity

This is where the teacher assesses accurately what is supposed to be assessed. The skills, knowledge and understanding have to match the learning objectives of a lesson or unit whilst also involving the use of reliable strategies to measure what is to be assessed. Children with SEN, for example, may struggle with the planning of movement sequences and not the execution of the skills, therefore the child may be hampered by not knowing what is occurring at particular points in time and consequently this needs to be taken into account.

Reliability

This should ensure consistency of measurement under the same conditions and it is important that the process is seen to be fair, so any teacher who makes an assessment would find the same result.

Objectivity

This is related to reliability in as much as the assessment should not reflect personal or institutional prejudices. This is where personal judgements and assumptions can creep in about specific children or how their conditions may impact on performance. It is therefore important to recognise this in order to minimise its impact on your judgements.

Practicality

Too many schemes of assessment are time consuming and take much-needed teaching and learning time away from PE lessons. Therefore, the teacher needs to find a practical blend between the demand for detailed assessment information and the practicality of the lesson.

According to Stillwell and Wilgoose (1997 adapted PE and assessment programmes for children with SEN serve the following purposes:

- **screening** – to determine which pupils are in need of help;
- **placement** – to ensure that each pupil needing help is in the proper environment;
- **diagnosis** – to determine the present level of performance of each pupil, to guide both the selection of activities and instruction;
- **progress** – to determine if the behavioural objectives have been met.

Conclusion

The importance of assessment has been clearly supported by many writers (Capel 2004, Piotrowski 2000). Yet, despite its importance, the quality and use of assessment data, particularly in physical education, was an area of concern according to the OFSTED (2002) annual report, with only one in ten schools being judged 'good' in terms of PE assessment. The explanation behind this suggests that weaknesses are a consequence of poor or inefficient planning, and a lack of specific objectives against which pupils' work will be assessed. Furthermore, teachers are often preoccupied with what pupils have to do, as opposed to what they are supposed to learn (OFSTED 2002). Assessment should focus upon what pupils learn and how well they learn it. This information then becomes the basis for future planning and provides teachers with vital information on their own performance as a teacher.

Carroll (1994) implies that assessment always involves making a judgement. Assessment does not simply record what pupils have done in a lesson, but also makes some sort of qualitative statement as well. Whilst there is a wide choice of different assessment procedures, these need to be decided on the basis of the purpose for which the assessment is being undertaken.

This may well mean employing different techniques for different assessment purposes.

The first role of assessment is to improve teaching and learning. Assessment can give feedback to children, which can help them progress, and also allows the teacher to evaluate their effectiveness by assessing how well the learning objectives have been achieved. Learning objectives are specific statements, which set out exactly what you want the children to learn. They form the intention or purpose of the lesson and are realised through the content selected and the learning experiences given to the pupils. Assessment can also indicate the nature and level of a child's achievement at specific points in their school life – for example, a level from the NC for PE (2000) grade descriptors. Assessment can also be used for diagnostic purposes; this is especially important in detecting special needs in particular areas. It can also help to identify strengths and weaknesses, which will inform planning and teaching.

It is hoped that in this chapter it has become apparent that learning and assessment go hand-in-hand. In other words, if we teach children a basic movement pattern it is necessary for the teacher to assess the child's ability to perform the task. If the task is shown to be meaningful to the child and will enhance their everyday lives then the assessment and feedback become very important. This is imperative to all teachers if learning is to progress and movement patterns and motor skills are to develop.

Chapter 6

Teaching and learning strategies

Introduction and context

It is recognised that learning has cognitive, social and emotional dimensions. Consequently, teachers need to think about how to develop intellectual and mental representational skills alongside consideration of the social environment within which learning takes place and the individual needs of the child. Pupils with SEN, like their non-disabled peers, learn in different ways and it is important to acknowledge that this is affected by relationships with teachers. Thus, in order for effective learning and engagement to take place, teachers need to have a sound grasp of a wide array of issues and concepts in order to maximise children's physical, social, intellectual and emotional development.

In beginning to examine children's educational development there are four basic elements which impact on learning – are social contexts, knowledge, the curriculum and psychological issues. In order to begin to address the needs of children with SEN and/or their non-disabled peers it is vital that teachers have a thorough appreciation of the potential impact they can have on the success or otherwise of a child's learning and development. These can be described as follows:

- **Social contexts** look at the relationship between teaching and learning environments and the ideological thinking and philosophical approaches of the time such as the NC, school culture, local community contexts and the individual needs of children.
- **Knowledge** has a significant impact on the types of teaching strategies used and pupils' development of their learning. For example, children have different levels of knowledge, understanding and needs which should be accommodated within every lesson by the teacher.
- **The curriculum** directs the nature and content of the specific subjects and whole school approaches which are often required as part of a statutory educational process. However, this still requires teachers to make professional judgements on the interpretation of the curriculum.

- **Psychological issues** refer to the wide and diverse range of theoretical approaches that can be applied to teaching and learning and the discussion and reflection that needs to be part of a teacher's professional role. Furthermore, this requires teachers to be aware of new theoretical approaches that may arise and be ready to trial and apply them as necessary.

Task 6.1 The four elements of teaching

Look at the four elements of teaching above and consider what these mean to you, and what strategies you would need to employ when working specifically with children with SEN in PE.

According to Kyriacou (1986), learning is a change in behaviour as a result of being engaged in an educational experience. In order to consider how learning occurs in children there are many theories which have been proposed. For example, Piaget (1962) argues that children pass through stages before they gain the ability to perceive reason and understand what is going on. As a result, it is suggested that children go through sequential stages of development and that their thinking is very different to that of adults. Thus Piaget would argue that teachers need to recognise the various stages of educational development that children are at as well as recognise the differences in thinking that children will have to interpret particular learning situations.

In contrast Vygotsky (1962) shares part of Piaget's views, but stresses the importance of activity as the fundamental basis for learning. A key element of Vygotsky's theory is based around what he refers to as the zone of proximal development which focuses upon the gap between what children can know and do themselves, and what they need help to achieve. Consequently it is argued that children can learn experientially through active learning on their own and with others, but at some stage they will need specialist help to progress their learning to a higher plain.

Bruner's (1971) theory of social learning offers another perspective in which cultural social experience is seen as vital to children's development. As a result, all learning according to Bruner needs to take place as part of a wider social experience. This emphasises in particular the potential of the teacher and the environment in making or breaking success and development. This is of particular relevance to children with SEN in PE who need teachers to adopt flexible approaches to learning and be ready to respond to the individual needs that they present with.

Teaching styles can be described as methods of learning and experiencing which are built from a strategy that also combines the individual behaviour of the teacher. A range of teaching and learning styles can be employed, ranging from command styles (teacher-directed) through reciprocal teaching (children working together) to a variety of self-teaching styles where people learn

Task 6.2 Theories of learning
Using the table below review your understanding of the theories of learning articulated by Piaget, Bruner and Vygotsky. You should look to develop your understanding of each theory and then relate it to children with SEN in PE.

Learning theory	Your understanding of the theory	What is the relationship of the theory to including children with SEN in PE?
Piaget		
Vygotsky		
Bruner		

independently (see Mosston and Ashworth 1994). This continuum of teaching styles (and the range and differences that comprise different styles) are critical to matching the pupil and teacher experience together to ensure a successful outcome. In contrast to teaching styles are learning styles, which basically describe the manner in which people's brains store information. Consequently there is a wide range of learning styles and the critical factor to consider in ensuring effective learning is that teachers adapt their styles to the needs of specific learners and groups.

The range of learning styles

There are many different ways to classify learning styles, which fall into general categories of perceptual modality, information processing, and personality patterns. The categories represent the different ways in which teachers focus their attention on the learner and can be described as follows:

- **Perceptual modalities** define biologically based reactions to our physical environment and represent the way children most efficiently adopt information. Teachers should help children to learn their perception style so that they can seek out information in the format that they process it most directly.
- **Information processing** distinguishes between the way children sense, think, solve problems, and remember information. Each child will have a preferred, consistent and distinct way of perceiving, organising and retaining information and it is vital that teachers grasp the individual differences in order to aid learning.

- **Personality patterns** focus on attention, emotion and values. By appreciating these differences teachers are able to predict the way children will react and feel about different situations.

Although there is a range of theories on learning styles they can be grouped into three sensory types, auditory, tactile and visual, from which most other styles can be seen as related extensions.

- **Auditory learners** learn through listening (which may have increased significance if a child has a visual impairment), verbal lectures, discussions, talking things through, and listening to what others have to say. Auditory learners interpret the underlying meanings of speech through listening to tone of voice, pitch, speed and other nuances.
- **Tactile/kinaesthetic learners** learn through moving, doing, and touching. These children learn best from a hands-on approach whereby they actively explore the physical world around them. They tend to find it hard to sit still for long periods and may become distracted by their need for activity and exploration.
- **Visual learners** learn through seeing (which is essential to children who may have learning difficulties or hearing impairments). These learners need to see the teacher's body language and facial expression to fully understand the content of a lesson. They tend to prefer sitting at the front of the classroom to avoid visual obstructions (e.g. people's heads). They may think in pictures and learn best from visual displays including diagrams, illustrated text books, overhead transparencies, videos, flipcharts and hand-outs.

Task 6.3 Sensory learning

Review your understanding of auditory, tactile/kinaesthetic and visual learners, and consider how you could use this knowledge when including children with SEN in PE.

In support of the three basic sensory types, Kolb's model of learning (1976) is based around four aspects of:

- **reflective observation** – helping children to gain meaning and orientation to the activity they are going to participate in;
- **abstract conceptualisation** – giving children orientation to the theoretical concepts which underpin the activity;
- **concrete experience** – helping children towards solution-oriented experiences;

- **active experimentation** – in which children are oriented towards the activity in order to experience and learn from this.

In analysing Kolb's learning styles there is a clear process of children moving through stages of observation, understanding concepts, looking for solutions, then experimenting through practice to learn and develop. For some children with SEN particular stages may have more meaning and emphasis than others and this needs to be taken into account by the teacher. For example, a child with a visual impairment will not rely so much on reflective observation, but will need to have further support with understanding the physical movement concepts that are required to perform a particular skill. Consequently the key to successful learning experiences lies in the ability of the teacher to recognise how children learn best in relation to their needs.

Gardiner's theory of learning styles (1988)

In addition to the work of Kolb, Gardiner's learning styles are based around what is often described as multiple intelligences based upon identifying seven different ways of children demonstrating their intellectual ability. This again is a key focus for teachers to consider, particularly when working with children with SEN as part of them demonstrating their knowledge and understanding of a subject in a manner which suits their specific needs. The seven styles are as follows:

- **Verbal and/or linguistic intelligence** is concerned with the ability to use words and language. These learners have highly developed auditory skills and are generally articulate speakers. They tend to think in words rather than pictures and their skills include listening, speaking, writing, story-telling, explaining, using humour, understanding the syntax and meaning of words, remembering information, convincing someone of their point of view, and analysing language usage.
- **Mathematical intelligence** is concerned with the ability to use reason, logic and numbers. These children think conceptually in logical and numerical patterns, making connections between pieces of information, and are always curious about the world around them. In addition they tend to ask lots of questions and like to do experiments. Their skills include problem solving, classifying and categorising information, working with abstract concepts to figure out the relationship of each to the other, handling long chains of reason to make local progressions, doing controlled experiments, questioning and wondering about natural events, performing complex mathematical calculations and working with geometric shapes.
- **Visual/spatial intelligence** refers to the ability to perceive visual images, and these children tend to think in pictures and need to create vivid

mental images to retain information. They enjoy looking at maps, charts, pictures, videos, and movies and their skills include puzzle building, reading, writing, understanding charts and graphs, sense of direction, sketching, painting, creating visual metaphors and analogies (perhaps through the visual arts), manipulating images, constructing, fixing, designing practical objects and interpreting visual images.

- **Bodily/kinaesthetic intelligence** refers to the ability to control body movements and handle objects skilfully. These learners express themselves through movement and have a good sense of balance and hand–eye co-ordination (for example, ball play, balancing beams). Through interacting with the space around them, they are able to remember and process information, and their skills include dancing, physical co-ordination, sport, hands-on experimentation, using body language, crafts, acting, miming, using their hands to create or build, and expressing emotions through the body.

- **Musical/rhythmic intelligence** refers to the ability to produce and appreciate music and these children are often inclined to think in sounds, rhythms and patterns. They immediately respond to music, either by appreciating or criticising what they hear, with many of the learners being extremely sensitive to environmental sounds. Their skills are focused upon singing, whistling, playing musical instruments, recognising tonal patterns, composing music, remembering melodies and understanding the structure and rhythm of music.

- **Interpersonal intelligence** relates to an ability to relate to and understand others, with such children trying to see things from other people's point of view in order to understand how they think and feel. They often have the ability to sense feelings, intentions and motivations and are great organisers, although they sometimes resort to manipulation. Generally they try to maintain peace in group settings and encourage co-operation whilst using both verbal (for example, speaking) and non-verbal (for example, eye contact, body language) language to open communication channels with others. Their skills include seeing things from other perspectives (dual-perspective), listening, using empathy, understanding other people's moods and feelings, counselling, co-operating with groups, noticing people's moods, motivations and intentions, communicating both verbally and non-verbally, building trust, peaceful conflict resolution and establishing positive relations with other people.

- **Intrapersonal intelligence** refers to the ability to self-reflect and be aware of one's inner state of being. These learners try to understand their inner feelings, dreams, relationships with others, and strengths and weaknesses. Their skills include recognising their own strengths and weaknesses, reflecting and analysing themselves, awareness of their inner feelings, desires and dreams, evaluating their thinking patterns, reasoning with themselves and understanding their role in relationship to others.

In summary, by teachers having an appreciation of the variety of intelligences that children may demonstrate it offers the potential for children to maximise their learning and development whilst giving them the best opportunities to demonstrate and gain knowledge and understanding in PE. This is critical with children with SEN, who may have particular intelligences which teachers can work through in order to tap into their learning behaviour and activities.

Teaching and learning in the context of children with SEN in PE

All teachers have their own natural teaching styles which are part of the diversity of PE experiences that can be presented to children with SEN. However, what is more important than an individual teacher's particular style of delivery is the ability to demonstrate a comprehensive range of teaching, learning and assessment strategies in order to be able to adapt and modify practice according to individual needs and specific class, activity or environmental needs. Thus, as we have the potential to teach in different ways, so children need to learn in different ways. This section of the chapter sets out to provide you with a range of teaching and learning strategies that you may wish to consider as part of the enhancement of your inclusive PE practice. In fact, it is important to recognise that if we as teachers can get better at delivering a range of teaching and learning styles it will benefit all children, and not just those with SEN.

PE has a distinctive role to play with children with SEN, as it does not just focus on the education of the physical, but it also has social, emotional, cognitive, moral and language dimensions as well. Consequently, a first step in the teaching and learning process is to consider the learning outcomes of the PE lesson. These could possibly be split into two categories, which focus upon principles of learning to move and moving to learn, which both have desirable outcomes for a child with SEN in PE.

Learning to move is an intrinsic benefit of PE and can be seen as the traditional outcome of a lesson. This is where teachers identify skills to be taught and learned by the pupils in a variety of contexts. This may have a particular focus if a child has movement difficulties in PE, and outcomes may be modified to accommodate this need.

Moving to learn is where outcomes are based more on the result of experiences rather than a focus on the quality of movement and/or specific physical skills. This can be described as more of an extrinsic benefit and PE offers many opportunities for developing pupils' co-operation, empathy, team work, leadership skills and so on. The objectives here tend to be more immediate and can be very specific to an individual child's needs. For example, if a child needs to learn how to take turns or listen to the views of others, this can be set up as a specific outcome for the child to work on. This will naturally

Task 6.4 Learning to move, and moving to learn
Read again the descriptors related to the concepts of learning to move, and moving to learn. Then use the table below to summarise a range of strategies that would accommodate this type of learning outcome in PE lessons.

Objective	Strategies to employ to meet the specific context within which learning will take place
Learning to move	
Moving to learn	

have wider social benefits than the PE context if, for instance, a child learns to be more accommodating with their behaviour when with others.

Planning and delivering your teaching and learning

The issues related to the planning, organisation, delivery and review of your teaching and learning in many ways are just the same for children with SEN as they are for other children. Consequently if we are to make attempts at improving our mixed ability teaching this will benefit all pupils within our classes and potentially make us better teachers. The distinction comes, however, in the specific nature of how you as the teacher can address the individual needs of children with SEN. It is often the case that only minor changes to your teaching, learning and assessment will be required to accommodate children with SEN in order for them to gain their full entitlement and accessibility to the PE curriculum. However, the question that is often posed is, where do I start in considering the needs of children with SEN in PE? A good starting point is to make a list of what information and issues you are likely to need to know about in order to address the needs of specific children within specific activity and environmental contexts. This list could include ensuring that as part of your planning you have:

- collected up-to-date medical information;
- consulted with teachers, parents and pupils;
- established class routines;
- read individual education plans;
- been open to modification of teaching and learning outcomes;
- considered assessment strategies.

Grouping and support in the PE lesson

A central issue to the success or otherwise of your PE lesson and the experience gained by the child is that you have taken into account the grouping and support that may be required in particular contexts. Thus, you will need to carefully consider each part of the lesson plan and organisation, and anticipate whether children are best working individually, reciprocally and/or in large groups. If you consider these issues in advance it can make a major difference in the success of your learning activity, whilst constantly bearing in mind the need to still be flexible and open to modifying activities as you progress through them.

It is worth considering that in any typical PE class you will have children who are on a diverse continuum of learning needs. Consequently, groups need to be carefully matched according to their confidence and skill level, and the nature of the activity being delivered. It is important to remember, however, that it is not necessary always to group people according to physical ability. There are many examples in which a child who struggles with physical competence can be paired with someone who is more careful and both can be equally stretched and receive their full entitlement to the curriculum. For example, a child with cerebral palsy who may struggle to send and receive a ball could be paired with a competent ball-thrower. The proficient ball-thrower will have to work on precision, accuracy and weighting of the ball to ensure the other child has the best success in receiving the ball, whilst the variety of sending that may be returned by the child with cerebral palsy will help the proficient child to be adaptable to changing sending patterns.

In other PE contexts it may, however, be more advantageous to pair pupils of similar ability together. This would be the case in gymnastic or dance activities where, if they are working on sequencing or mirroring work, the pupils will be working at a similar level to each other. Other grouping contexts, such as competitive activities, need to be given careful consideration. When pupils are working on small-scale skill development they often work well and function at their own levels. However, in large group settings difference often presents itself at the most extreme. As a result it may be better to group people who are at similar physical and emotional levels, or work specifically on ensuring that all team members have a role to play that is appropriate to their needs.

Task 6.5 Grouping pupils

Reflect upon the comments in relation to grouping pupils and consider what issues and challenges you may face when dealing with children who are working on a diverse continuum of learning needs.

If a child has a formal Statement of SEN there may or may not be an element of learning assistant support available, but this will depend on the individual needs and circumstances of the child and school context. It is important, though, to ensure that if you feel support is required you discuss this with the SENCO to work out strategies for accommodating any particular support arrangements. Whilst a learning support assistant is there to help the child, it is important to recognise that you are still responsible for the planning, organisation and delivery of that child's PE lesson. Consequently you are responsible for guiding and working with the support assistant to ensure the child gets the best experience possible. It is also important to recognise that often the support assistant will spend the majority of the day with one child and will be a valuable resource to you in developing your planning and organisation.

In addition to the support of a learning assistant there are many other methods of support that a child with SEN may need. These may include:

- help in breaking down tasks to smaller constituent parts to aid explanation and understanding;
- providing specific feedback to pupils with particular contexts (particularly if the child has learning difficulties, or sensory needs);
- physical support if a child has restricted ranges of movement;
- repeating instructions and offering further guidance in order to make it more meaningful;
- adapting the nature of the outcomes or activity (for example changes to rules, equipment and so on).

Developing strategies for task adaptation

Changing the nature of the task to accommodate individual children with SEN requires careful thought and planning in order to be effective. This may involve changes to rules, equipment, tasks and the like in order to ensure full accessibility to the activity. This may not mean significant changes to the task, and you often will find that only minor modifications will make a substantial difference to the accessibility and entitlement that child receives. For example, offering children a selection of different ball sizes or equipment with shorter or longer handles often results in them naturally selecting the equipment they are most comfortable with. Furthermore, you can change the rules to ensure some pupils have more time on the ball or all have to receive a pass before scoring. Placing pupils into their own zones and territories is another method of adapting the task to accommodate different needs.

The most important issue to bear in mind when adapting tasks is that you ensure that:

- any modification and adaptation to the task does not affect its integrity and is not patronising or tokenistic;
- accessibility to the PE lessons remains the responsibility of the teacher, in consultation with support assistants and pupils where necessary;
- any modifications to an activity do not affect its curriculum relevance;
- any modification to small-sided or modified activities should be planned with the intention of moving to the full activity and with the use of full equipment if possible;
- children have an entitlement to access the PE curriculum and it is the school's responsibility to deliver this.

An important aspect of planning work with children with SEN is the need to consider the most appropriate methods of breaking the tasks down to smaller constituent parts. Here the teacher will need to consider the child's physical, intellectual, emotional and social needs as part of the organisation and development of activities. As a result, in order for the child to progress, careful consideration of what stage each pupil's learning and development is at is essential if meaningful and successful participation is to take place. Part of this will require some consultation with the child in order that they know what is being expected of them.

Task 6.6 Adapting tasks
Look at the issues around adapting tasks discussed above. Using the table below consider how you would ensure you address these issues within your teaching and learning activity with children with SEN.

Aspect of adaptation	Strategies to ensure delivery
Maintaining integrity	
Accessibility is the responsibility of the teacher	
Keeping activities relevant to the curriculum	
Ensuring entitlement to the PE curriculum	

Guidelines to inclusive teaching and learning approaches

Whilst there are no definitive protocols to follow when planning, organising and delivering inclusive PE there are certain fundamental principles that will help you develop entitlement and accessibility in your lessons. Applying these principles will act as a focus for your reflection in ensuring that any differentiated practices also offer integrity, which is vital to enabling children to feel comfortable and confident in their PE experiences. These include:

- **organisational adaptations** such as the physical location of the learning environment – this is of particular importance if you are working with children with mobility needs, where physical accessibility may be a particular problem;
- **support arrangements** before, during and after the lesson;
- **grouping and organisation** of pupils within the lessons according to individual need and learning context;
- **variety of teaching styles**, involving a readiness to change and adapt to meet the needs of individual learners;
- **attention to the breaking down of tasks** to ensure children have a clear awareness of and guidance on what is being expected of them;
- **differentiated assessment strategies** that act to prevent barriers to children demonstrating their knowledge, understanding and learning to date;
- **matching the activity** to the levels of children in order to ensure learning and development;
- **modification to equipment** including rules, equipment, height, colours, weights and textures of resources;
- **modifications to space** including the use of zoning.

Conclusion

The development of effective teaching, learning and assessment strategies is critical for the effective inclusion of children with SEN in PE. As part of creating effective processes, teachers need to be committed to developing flexibility in their pedagogical practices whilst responding positively to the need to modify and adapt strategies and style to meet the needs of individual learners. A central aspect of this comes through recognition of social models of disability, in which it is the teacher's and school's responsibility to change what they are doing to accommodate children with SEN, rather than the other way round.

Chapter 7

Multi-disciplinary approaches and working in partnership

Introduction and context

The 1997 government report *Excellence for All Children* (DfEE 1997a) high-lighted a need to improve the consistency of SEN provision across the country, so that every child gets the best education available, regardless of where they live. To help make this happen, the DfES set up 11 SEN regional partnerships, to help local authorities and other providers work together so they can share experience and knowledge and, where possible, plan and develop services as a region, rather than individually. The need for agencies to work in partnership through multi-disciplinary approaches is a vital element in ensuring that children with SEN and their teachers receive the best support, advice and guidance required to produce successful learning and participation.

The SEN regional partnerships' main task is to help resolve the problem of variations in SEN services across the country, so that the services available to children do not depend on where they live. One of the main ways of doing this is to bring together all those involved in SEN in a particular region, so they can share expertise and experience, learn from each other's successes, identify gaps in provision and plan how to fill them.

By promoting this regional approach to planning and provision, the part-nerships are helping to make sure that:

- the right SEN services are available to those who need them;
- services are provided as efficiently as possible;
- examples of best practice can be learned from and extended;
- local and regional expertise is being used to inform central government policy making.

The partnerships have also been asked by the DfES to spend at least 60 per cent of their time on:

- developing more inclusive policies and practices;

- improving the effectiveness of SEN processes and services;
- making sure that government initiatives are put into practice;
- strengthening co-operation between different agencies.

As a result, if agencies and individual practitioners work together to support the educational development of children with SEN through holistic approaches this will contribute to aiding their social, physical, emotional and intellectual needs both within and outside of school. This chapter sets out to examine the roles that some professionals play in supporting teachers and children with SEN and to state the case for working in partnership rather than in isolation as a means to successful and meaningful participation and engagement in PE.

Task 7.1 Multi-agency working

Review what you see as the advantages and potential disadvantages and challenges of taking a multi-disciplinary partnership approach to the inclusion of children with SEN in PE.

Defining partnerships

Partnerships can be described as arrangements between two or more parties who have agreed to work co-operatively towards shared and/or compatible objectives and in which there is shared authority and responsibility; joint investment of resources; shared liability or risk-taking; and, ideally, mutual benefits. Taken together, these definitions suggest the following four key elements which distinguish and define partnerships:

- common objectives and goals among partners (objectives may be the impetus of the partnership or they may evolve over time);
- shared risk and mutual benefits (risks and benefits may be different for each partner and may accrue with different timeframes);
- contributions from both partners (including both monetary and non-monetary);
- shared authority, responsibility and accountability.

Underlying many of these definitions is also the notion that the partnership represents, to all partners, a better strategy to address a specific project or goal than each partner operating independently. In other words, the partnership is considered to add value to the efforts of the individual partners. This is certainly the case when working with children with SEN, who may have a range of needs that have to be addressed. Consequently a central feature of successful inclusion is the commitment and desire for multi-agency and partnership working approaches. For example, a child who has restricted ranges of movement may well need the services of a physiotherapist who can support the child with extending and developing physical activity safely. As a result, the lesson can support any remedial work that is done, but at the same time physiotherapy should not be seen as a replacement for PE. Children still need and deserve their entitlement to the activities of the PE NC, and working with physiotherapists within the curriculum can only aid school and wider lifestyle experience and involvement.

The SEN toolkit and strategic involvement of partners

The SEN toolkit, mainly for schools and LEAs, contains practical advice on how to implement the *Code of Practice* introduced in January 2002. This toolkit identifies the importance of partnership working, particularly in relation to social and health services. As part of the requirements of the toolkit it is stated that social service departments should give LEAs information on the range of services that are generally available for families of children 'in need'. This partnership approach between education and social services ensures that information on planning processes, data collection and specific local arrangements for the early identification of children who they think may have special educational needs are provided. The information that social services may provide to education authorities that would be of specific relevance to PE could include data on young children with developmental difficulties, disabilities or particular medical conditions in order to ensure that schools are aware of their needs and able to effectively plan and arrange the necessary support to facilitate their inclusion. As a result, as part of their partnerships with education social services should:

- inform LEAs of children who they think may have SEN;
- provide advice to LEAs for the assessment of children within the statutory time limits of the *Code of Practice* on SEN;
- consider with LEAs the social services contribution to the non-educational provision to be specified in a statement;
- ensure all schools have a contact for seeking social work advice on children who may have SEN;
- provide a resource to social workers who require assistance in preparing reports for SEN statutory assessment;
- participate in multi-agency meetings on assessments and making statements;
- make sure that there are appropriate mechanisms so that social work advice is provided for annual review meetings and transition planning when appropriate.

Involvement of health services

Health authorities should have arrangements for ensuring local primary care trusts and general practitioners have the necessary information to support children with SEN and their relationship to the wider educational process. Authorities should as part of the SEN toolkit be able to state what the arrangements for the early identification of children with particular difficulties are, and whether they think they may have SEN. Specific information that health authorities can be of help with in relation to PE includes identifying young children with physical, sensory, developmental difficulties or particular medical conditions. Thus health authorities, as part of their partnership with education authorities, should seek to:

- ensure that all schools have a contact (usually the school health service) for seeking medical advice on children who may have SEN;
- provide a resource to other health service staff – for example, doctors and therapists – who require assistance in preparing reports on the medical history and health needs of children for schools and LEAs;
- co-ordinate the health services' advice for a statutory assessment and, frequently, participate in multi-agency meetings on assessments and making statements;
- co-ordinate the provision to be made by the health services for a child with SEN;
- in some circumstances be responsible for the purchasing of these services;
- make sure that there are appropriate mechanisms so that health advice is provided for annual review meetings and transition planning when appropriate.

Task 7.2 Partnership approaches to SEN in PE
Using the table below review your understanding of the roles of health, education and social services in terms of what services, advice and guidance they can offer to each other and what the benefits are likely to be to you as the teacher and the child with SEN.

Authority	What is your understanding of the role of each agency?	What are the benefits of collaborative working for the teacher of children with SEN in PE?
Social services		
Health authorities		
Education authorities		

Holistic approaches and the role of specialists

One of the central components of successful inclusion is the ability of a wide range of professionals to work together to provide a co-ordinated support service to specific children with SEN. In relation to PE, taking an holistic approach to children with SEN is vital if teachers are to be aware of all the needs and issues that may face them, and have the resources, information and guidance to be in a position to take appropriate action. As a result, the types of support teachers are likely to need when supporting children with SEN in PE are those from specialists such as physiotherapists, occupational therapists, educational psychologists, nurses, speech and language therapists and sometimes disability governing bodies of sport. In drawing together this multi-disciplinary team of professionals, the knowledge and understanding that can be gained by teachers in order to give a comprehensive understanding of child with SEN is critical. Furthermore, teachers will help to ensure that they provide a co-ordinated and whole-person centred approach to the specific needs of children, by listening to and reflecting upon the advice and guidance given by each professional.

In relation to the role of occupational therapists, in order for them to qualify and practice they are required to have a thorough appreciation of aspects of anatomy, physiology, neurology, and psychology in order to assist with the assessment and support of children with functional difficulties. These therapists are primarily of use to teachers and children in that they have specific skills in observation and activity analysis and the implementation of carefully graded activities to develop, learn or re-learn skills to foster independent living. Furthermore, and with specific relevance to supporting children with SEN in PE, paediatric occupational therapists' knowledge of neurology, child development and cognitive psychology offers teachers an insight into the understanding of gross and fine motor skills and movement in order to help them plan effective educational programmes.

In contrast, physiotherapists have knowledge and appreciation of anatomy and physiology, and are experts in analysing movement. They are particularly focused around aspects of the examination of children's movement based on the structure and function of the body and physical approaches to promoting health, preventing injury, treatment and rehabilitation, and the management of particular disability conditions. Consequently, in relation to supporting children with SEN in PE physiotherapists can help teachers to improve the quality and ranges of movement that are central to successful learning and participation.

Speech and language therapists offer essential information in helping children who have speech errors and communication and language development. They are of particular importance to teachers of PE in helping them to ensure children are able to communicate and interact in effective ways with their peers and tutors. In addition, teachers can, through PE, reinforce any particular language programmes that are being worked on with a child with SEN.

Educational psychologists focus on the study of learning outcomes, student attributes, and instructional processes which directly relate to the classroom and the school. In addition they can support pupils and teachers in ensuring that individual needs are clearly understood, then plan for effective and supportive educational programmes. As part of the statutory assessment of SEN under the *Code of Practice*, an educational psychologist helps gather information for teachers, parents and professional support agencies. They also assist in evaluating children's thinking abilities and assessing individual strengths and weaknesses. Together, the parents, teachers, and educational psychologist formulate plans to help children learn more effectively and are critical to the co-ordinated and multi-disciplinary partnership approaches to the support of children with SEN in PE.

Task 7.3 The role of therapists

Using the table below, outline in your own words what you see as the different roles therapists play in supporting children with SEN. You should then relate this specifically to how these therapists can support you as a teacher to ensure you have a full grasp of the individual needs of children with SEN and how they relate to PE.

Therapist	Your understanding of their role	How can these therapists support teachers in PE?
Occupational therapists		
Physiotherapist		
Speech and language therapist		
Educational psychologist		

Concluding thoughts on the importance of multi-disciplinary and partnership approaches

Increasingly within education you are likely to see multi-disciplinary partnership approaches to ensuring that children with SEN gain their full entitlement and accessibility to the PE curriculum. Consequently it is vital that teachers have a thorough understanding of the range of services that are on offer to support both children and teachers alike. What is critical in ensuring that these partnerships are effective is that each professional values and appreciates the individual role that each can offer to the child and each other in ensuring children with SEN receive the best support, care and education possible. In addition to the standard health and education therapists it may be appropriate for teachers to make contact with local disability sports clubs and national governing bodies in order to assist with children's development outside the formal school curriculum. Again this is a critical element of not only supporting children with SEN as part of the curriculum, but also ensuring that they have access to agencies that can assist with their lifelong participation in physical activity outside of school.

Consequently, teachers' commitment to holistic and multi-disciplinary partnership approaches is essential if children with SEN are to learn and progress in their PE lessons. It is hoped that in this short chapter the discussion has gone some way to encouraging you to extend your understanding of other professional roles and how they can support children to have a positive PE experience.

Chapter 8

Opportunities outside the curriculum

Introduction and context

Although the focus of this book has largely been on core curriculum matters in inclusive PE, it is important to highlight how pupils with SEN can access activity outside the curriculum time through extra-curricular and/or community based activities. This is of particular relevance as the PE NC (QCA 1999a) makes direct links with school and extra-curricula sporting activities, which children with SEN are just as entitled to as their non-disabled peers. There are a number of organisations and initiatives aimed at providing activity for children alongside those specialist agencies who support children with SEN. Consequently, as part of their extended inclusive practice PE teachers should seek to develop partnership links with such organisations. This is of particular relevance in the Government's *Game Plan* (DCMS 2002) strategy, which encourages school–community links in order to ensure that the foundations of physical activity within the curriculum are built upon and extended after school into lifelong enjoyment and participation in sport.

In addition, with the Government's health agenda and concerns over increases in childhood obesity the health of the nation's young children, including those with SEN, is a key area for action. Figures produced by the Department of Health (DH 2005) reveal a steady rise in obesity among children in England. The figures, which have tracked children under age 11 from 1995 to 2003, show that 27.7 per cent of children in England are overweight, with 13.7 per cent being described as obese. Lack of physical activity in childhood is linked intrinsically to obesity-related diseases in later life. However, through a combination of a healthy diet and regular physical activity from an early age, young people can radically reduce their chances of developing long-term illnesses such as diabetes and heart disease. A key component of fostering lifelong physical activity and healthy lifestyles is PE teachers, who have a duty to raise children's awareness of these issues and help children to create links with after school and community organisations to continue participation outside of the formal school curriculum. Research has shown, for example, that everyone should try to include at least 30 minutes of moderate physical activity in their lives, five times a week – with children taking part in 60 minutes of activity every day of the week.

In addition to the Government's drive to have a healthier nation of young people, the need to formalise links between the PE school curriculum, extra-curricular activity and community based sports organisations is essential in the drive to create lifelong participation. The national PE, School Sport and Club Links (PESSCL) strategy was launched by the Prime Minister in October 2002 and went live in April 2003 with the Government investing £978m. between 2003–04 and 2007–08 to deliver the strategy. In addition, a further £686m. lottery funding is enhancing school sports facilities, which means that in total over £1½ billion is being invested in PE and school sport in the UK during the five years up to 2008.

The DfES and the DCMS are working in partnership to lead the strategy, with its overall objective of enhancing the take-up of sporting opportunities by 5- to 16-year-olds. The targets are ambitious, with the aim to increase the percentage of school children who spend a minimum of two hours a week on high-quality PE and school sport within and beyond the curriculum to 75 per cent by 2006 and then 85 per cent by 2008. The long-term ambition, by 2010, is to offer all children at least four hours of sport every week, made up of:

- at least two hours of high-quality PE and sport at schools – with the expectation that this will be delivered totally within the curriculum;
- an additional two to three hours beyond the school day, delivered by a range of school, community and club providers.

In addition, the Government's *Youth Matters* (DfES 2005) paper on providing **opportunity, challenge** and **support** to young people seeks to ascertain views on how to reform services in England, including sports activities for young people (including those who have SEN). The proposals include setting new national standards for the activities that all young people would benefit from accessing in their free time and it is proposed that this will include access to two hours per week of sporting activity. The national strategy is being delivered through nine interlinked strands. These are:

- **specialist sports colleges,** in which schools specialise and offer a greater physical activity focus with the aim of enhancing whole school performance;
- **school sport partnerships,** which will create by 2006 a national PE and school sports infrastructure network of 400 colleges and partnerships (families of schools which work together). This is of particular importance in supporting children with SEN in schools where disability competition and participation may be restricted. Consequently, by schools linking

together more opportunities for children with specific needs and in particular sports can be achieved;

- **professional development** of teachers and coaches;
- **Step Into Sport,** involving support for children to engage in a range of sporting activities;
- **Club Links,** which aim to create links between schools and local community based clubs;
- **Gifted and Talented,** aiming to identify and support children including those with SEN who show potential in PE and school sport to excel;
- ensuring **sporting playgrounds** are maintained and used as a vehicle for physical activity;
- **swimming;**
- the **QCA's PE and School Sport Investigation which** are the tools the schools and partnerships draw on to enable children to take up their two hour entitlement and move towards the 2010 ambition.

Task 8.1 The Youth Matters agenda
Reflect upon the initiatives described above in relation to your understanding of them and how you think they apply to children with SEN. Use the table below to identify any potential issues or challenges you can see in meeting this agenda with children with SEN.

National strategy/ initiative	What is your understanding of the key principles?	What issues and challenges do you see in meeting these for children with SEN?	How do you foresee any issues and challenges being overcome?
Game Plan (DCMS 2002) encouraging school community links			
Government health figures (DH 2005)			
PESSCL strategy (DfES/DCMS 2002)			
Youth Matters agenda (DfES 2005)			

The structure of disability sport

The structure of disability sport, like developments in PE for children with SEN, is evolving, and in 1997 Sport England's task force on the future of disability sport (Sport England 1997) recommended that disability sport be incorporated into the work of governing bodies of sport. There was a clear recognition, however, that this was not going to occur in the short term and that a considerable amount of work was going to have to be undertaken to achieve this objective. The EFDS was established in order to achieve the shift towards a more integrated approach to the provision of sport for children with SEN and disabled adults.

EFDS aims to expand sporting opportunities for disabled people and increase the numbers actively involved in sport. It also aims to ensure that people with disabilities are included in sporting opportunities, and to encourage a move towards more inclusive approaches of delivery. Its mission is to be the united voice of disability sport, seeking to promote inclusion and achieve equality of sporting opportunities for disabled people. As a result, EFDS intends to deliver this mission through a set of core principles:

- be a leader in the co-ordination of the development of disability sport in England;
- mainstream sporting opportunities for disabled people;
- unite partners/stakeholders with common goals and strategies;
- create an influential and common voice;
- enable community and sporting partners to deliver;
- promote the wider benefits of sport and physical activity;
- promote equal opportunities;
- facilitate positive change for all impairments;
- provide information and 'signposting';
- lobby key agencies such as government to increase funding to the wider EFDS membership;
- lobby key agencies such as government to firmly establish the disability sport and physical activity agenda within their own organisations.

There are currently nine EFDS regions, where teachers can access information about local and national opportunities, each comprising membership of seven national disability sports organisations (NDSOs). The NDSOs are structured around impairment-specific groups encompassing: British Amputee and Les Autres Sports Association; British Blind Sport; British Deaf Sports Council; British Wheelchair Sports Foundation; Cerebral Palsy Sport; Disability Sport England and English Sports Association for People with Learning Disabilities. Whilst this reinforces the medical model of disability (Reiser and Mason 1990), the organisations have long-established traditions, and the aim over time is to function through mainstream governing bodies of sport, and one umbrella disability governing body (EFDS). This will be in line with current thinking on evolving inclusive practice within both sport and PE. In addition, by agencies such as EFDS working alongside mainstream governing bodies of sport, and schools, it is envisaged that inclusive activity has real potential for success in the future. Consequently it is crucial that PE teachers who support children with SEN have an in-depth appreciation of the extra-curricular and out of school sporting agencies that can support and develop lifelong physical activity participation.

Classification of disability sport and the history of the paralympic movement

According to Richter *et al.* (1992) classification systems have been widely used in sports to allow for fair and equitable starting points for competition. There is a distinction to be made, however, between definitions and rationales for 'medical' and 'functional' models of classification. Medical classifications are concerned with verifying minimum levels of disability, whilst a functional classification considers how an athlete performs in specific sports (Winnick 2000). Consequently, it is through functional classification that the structure of disability sport for competition purposes is organised. The functional classification, as Richter *et al.* (1992) indicate, establishes a starting point for fair competition that takes account of how disability impacts upon perfor-mance in specific sports. The functional classification is characterised by over 40 separate physical profiles, and three categories for people with visual impairments. This system, although complex in relation to disabled athletes gaining classification (through assessment by a medical practitioner), has worked well in relation to competition for individuals with a physical dis-ability (Depauw and Gavron 1995).

The situation is more complex, and less clear, when it comes to judgements on how 'intellectual cognition' relates to performance in sport, and this has been a subject of much debate at international level, at events such as the Paralympic Games. The Paralympic Games (parallel games) are the equiva-lent of the Olympic Games, but are mainly concerned with provision for the physically disabled and those with visual impairments. Deaf people com-pete in the World Deaf Games, whilst people with learning disabilities have the Special Olympics and a separate Paralympic movement. This categorised and distinctive organisational approach has served disability sport well over the years. However, in light of more recent moves to inclusive environments there is significant debate on how this should be reflected in relation to com-petition for disabled groups and individuals. Consequently, whilst in school sport and PE the shift is currently towards inclusive activity, there will always be a place for disability sports activity through which children with SEN can compete on relatively even playing fields. As a result, teachers will need to

---

Task 8.2 Researching disability sport organisations

Take time to undertake some research into organisations such as the English Federation for Disability Sport and the British Paralympic Association. You may even wish to talk to your local sport development officer to gain a more localised picture of the specific arrangements for disability sport. Once you have done this, reflect upon how these agencies can help you become an effective teacher in making links between the formal school PE curriculum and lifelong physical activity.

---

have a full appreciation of the structures of disability sport and the nature of classification systems if they are to enable children with SEN to access these structures.

The development of the Paralympic movement and disability sport is well documented (Depauw and Gavron 1995, Auxter 2001, Winnick 2000), with international competition in disability sport starting in 1948 at Stoke Mandeville as part of the 14th Olympic Games held in London. The background to the development of the Stoke Mandeville games was to include sport as part of a rehabilitation process for people with spinal cord injuries. This was within the context of innovatory practice, which acknowledged that disabled people could still participate and compete in sport (and at high levels) despite any limiting mobility factors. The first Paralympics were held in Rome in 1960 and have developed and increased in size significantly, culminating in the largest games in Sydney 2000. It was in Sydney that for the first time some disability events were held as part of the mainstream Olympic Games (which again was the case in Athens in 2004) whilst the separate Paralympics had regular crowd attendances of 90,000 spectators. This demonstrated the interest and recognition of how far disability sport had come in recent years and reinforces the shift towards more inclusive approaches to sport and PE. In addition, there are many lessons to be learned from countries such as Australia in fostering and developing the passion and interest in both physical participation and spectator sport which resulted in the largest attendances at any Paralympic games to date.

Finding local opportunities and creating school–community links

There are two key pathways that can be followed in the development of school–community links for children with SEN as part of an extension to the formal PE curriculum – disability-specific sports clubs, or mainstream sports clubs (Vickerman *et al.* 2003). As part of Sport England's strategies for sport over a long period of time, most local authorities have established sports development officers who know where local sports clubs meet, and how accessible they are to disabled people. Some local authorities produce directories of sports clubs that provide opportunities for disabled people, and sports development officers can act as invaluable links between school PE departments and local sports communities.

Governing bodies of sport, in line with Sport England's Disability Task Force (Sport England 1997), are taking a more inclusive approach to their delivery. Initiatives such as the Amateur Swimming Association's Swim 21 programme have ensured that disabled swimmers can access local swimming groups. EFDS's Ability Counts programme has worked with the Football Association to ensure that professional clubs include young disabled people in their community programmes, and local sports disability groups provide a good way of bridging the link between school and the community. Development work in disability sport is mainly concentrating at present on providing disabled people with more choice on the range of activities that they can become involved in, within inclusive, adapted, and disability sport settings. Clearly there is still a considerable way to go before total inclusion and mainstreaming of disability sport is fully realised. It is easy to be critical, but it should be recognised that inclusion is becoming a reality (Depauw and Doll-Tepper 2000) and not just a possibility, and strategies such as those by Sport England, and the development of EFDS, are complementing similar work being undertaken within the PE curriculum. New initiatives such as the introduction of the Youth Sport Trust TOP Sportsability programmes have also added a new dimension to the area of inclusive PE provision. The equipment provided by the Youth Sport Trust has been aimed specifically at special schools and mainstream schools with pupils with SEN.

Whilst this equipment is aimed at young people with SEN, all young people can join in playing by the same rules as their disabled peers. In addition, five separate games were included in the equipment bag issued by the Youth Sport Trust, which can be used to help those pupils with severe disabilities. These games are known as boccia (a bowls-type game), table cricket, table hockey, polybat (an adapted version of table tennis), and goalball (a game played by visually impaired people). Four of these games have pathways for young people to go on and progress from recreational level through to national, international and Paralympic competition, which further supports the need to provide clear, consistent and achievable pathways for children with SEN to progress through in PE, school sport, and wider community sporting opportunities.

The tabletop games, although designed primarily to be played on a table tennis table, are versatile enough to be played at most tables. Polybat was designed for children with SEN who have control and co-ordination difficulties. The development of a glove bat has ensured that pupils who find it hard to grip a bat can handle the polybat, and therefore can still participate successfully. In addition, activities such as goal ball (a three-a-side game developed for visually impaired people) can involve sighted players in which everyone wears adapted goggles. This is an example of 'reverse inclusion' (Auxter *et al*. 2001, Winnick 2000), where sighted people can be included in a disability-specific game as part of a PE teacher's use of the 'inclusion spectrum' noted earlier.

Task 8.3 The findings from the Sport England Survey
Using the table below reflect upon the findings from the Sport England Survey (2000) in relation to disabled children's involvement in physical activity. You should try to identify what and why the issues exist, then consider how you could address these issues as part of your own practice.

Key issues from the Sport England (2000) survey	What issues exist, and why?	What strategies can you employ to address these issues and concerns?
Over a quarter of young disabled people had not taken part in sport more than ten times in the past year, compared with 6 per cent of non-disabled young people		
Over 56 per cent of young people with a disability had taken part in sport outside of school, compared with 87 per cent for the non-disabled population		
37 per cent of young people with a disability had taken part in sport during their lunch break, compared with 67 per cent of the overall population of young people.		

Although these activities go some way to addressing activity levels for people with disabilities, research undertaken by Sport England (2000) has highlighted some interesting differences in sports participation between people with disabilities and their non-disabled peers. For example, the research found that over a quarter of young disabled people had not taken part in sport more than ten times in the past year, compared with 6 per cent of non-disabled young people; over 56 per cent of young people with a disability had taken part in sport outside of school, compared with 87 per cent for the non-disabled population; 37 per cent of young people with a disability had taken part in sport during their lunch break, compared with 67 per cent of the over-all population of young people.

Thus, whilst more opportunities are being created for young disabled people to participate either recreationally or competitively in sport, for schools and their PE teachers it is important to know where and how to access the net-work of provision available at both local and/or national level. This situation could be improved through better-informed partnerships between school PE departments and disability organisations, both nationally and regionally, and should be seen as a developing role within a PE department's inclusive struc-tures (Vickerman *et al.* 2003).

Conclusion

It is important that all young people, whether they have SEN or not, have the opportunities to participate, develop and excel in PE, school sport and com-munity based lifelong physical activity. This is important for their social, mental and physical health and well-being. However, in order to ensure that children with SEN receive the same opportunities as their non-disabled peers it is essential that teachers take a dual approach, first by recognising specialist disability sports organisations, and second by encouraging main-stream organisations to support children as well. A central part of the success or otherwise, however, is the teacher of PE having a full grasp of some of the potential issues and barriers noted in this chapter and an appreciation of the local and national agencies that are available both for advice and support to pupils, parents, the school and you as the teacher.

Chapter 9

Key principles for including children with SEN in PE

Introduction

Throughout this book the primary purpose has been to provide you with a combination of opportunities to engage in personal reflection and professional enquiry from theoretical and practical standpoints. All of the tasks in the book have been structured to offer opportunities for critical debate and discussion. Teaching is a reflective process, and requires you to be a dynamic practitioner who is ready to constantly ask critical questions of what, why, where, how, and when teaching, learning and assessment should take place. Consequently, the relationship between understanding and explaining your practice must be viewed as a dynamic process involving the need to engage, reflect and review all elements of your professional role. What is important to remember is that you are an individual teacher with your own particular personality, characteristics and approach to teaching, which is what is so great about teaching.

However, whilst taking note and reflecting on your own style and approach to working to include children with SEN in PE, it is important to have an open mind, high expectations and a readiness to adapt your practice. It is hoped that the chapters in this book have offered you opportunities for clarity and reflection on these points. This chapter sets out to provide a brief overview of the key themes and principles that have been discussed in the previous chapters, whilst offering some context for structuring your work with children with SEN in PE.

A framework for including children with SEN in PE

Whilst the intention throughout this book has been to encourage you to think flexibly and openly about the diversity of methods by which you can include children with SEN in PE, there is always the danger that too much flexibility can leave you with a feeling of being lost and with no context or concepts to attach your thoughts to. As a result the 'Eight P' framework (Vickerman 2002) encourages stakeholders (whether they be trainee teachers, practising teachers, schools or those working in advisory, leadership or support capacities) to systematically work through a series of key aspects of inclusive PE provision for children with SEN in order to review and seek clarity in your practice. The Eight P model builds upon and extends already known concepts of policy, process and practice but contextualises these within the subject of SEN and PE. The outline of the method given below could be undertaken either by an individual stakeholder (i.e. trainee, qualified teacher, lecturer) or by agencies working singularly or collaboratively to extend and develop their practice.

The 'eight P' inclusive PE framework for including children with SEN in PE (Vickerman 2002)	
Philosophy	Understanding clearly what the principles, concepts and contexts of inclusion stand for and their relationship to children with SEN in PE.
Purposeful	Understanding the rationales behind strategies for including children with SEN in PE and how their entitlement and accessibility can be created.
Proactive	Being ready to identify challenges and solutions to issues and problems you may face within a context of taking flexible approaches and a desire to be innovative and creative with your practice.
Partnership	Recognising that inclusion needs to take place within a context of consultation and negotiation as part of an holistic approach to PE for children with SEN.
Process	Recognising that inclusion takes time and you may not get it right the first time, but being prepared to try out new strategies and learn from the experience of diversity of styles and experiences.
Policy	Recognising that having institutional policies on equality of opportunity and inclusion in PE will demonstrate commitment to and support for the principles of entitlement and accessibility. The key, however, to any policy on inclusion is the impact it has in making a difference, whether that is strategically or at a practical level.

continued on facing page

Pedagogy	Recognising that in any inclusive process the key aspect of most significance is the teaching, learning and assessment activity that takes place with the teacher and child with SEN. As part of this process teachers need to adopt flexible approaches, have high expectations and be prepared to modify and adapt as part of their pedagogical practice.
Practice	If individual stakeholders take note and discuss, reflect and debate on all the points above it offers the best chance of you making a difference to the child with SEN in working towards ensuring they gain successful PE experiences.

In explaining this framework further, the first feature to consider is a need to recognise the **philosophy** behind inclusion and its relationships to basic and fundamental human rights. This requires consideration of how human rights are supported as a society through statutory and non-statutory guidance such as the SEN and Disability Rights Act 2001 (DfES, 2001c), and the PE NC (2000) Statutory Inclusion Statement (QCA 1999a). Furthermore, it requires stakeholders to spend time engaging in understanding philosophical theories and principles, such as those advocated by Skrtic (1995), Ainscow (1999), Dyson (2001), Dyson and Millward (2000) and Reiser and Mason (1990) (discussed in earlier chapters) prior to consideration of how to apply these in practice. If we do not get this first and fundamental belief system in place and understand our and our government's philosophical approaches to inclusive education the potential to realise it in practice is severely constrained.

In order to facilitate these debates stakeholders must embrace a **purposeful** approach to fulfilling the requirements of inclusive PE. Time should be spent initially examining philosophical standpoints in order to gain a clear appreciation of the rationale and arguments behind inclusive education. For example, the Audit Commission (2002) suggests that at present the TTA (2002) 'Professional Standards Framework' (TTA 2002) does not satisfactorily address the wider contexts of SEN (i.e. philosophical standpoints). Consequently, stakeholders should be resolute in ensuring they examine philosophical issues and how they feed into the wider inclusion debate. Thus we must as practitioners or policy makers be ready to ask questions about past, present and future practices and the relevance of them to the successful inclusion of children with SEN in PE.

In order to achieve these recommendations stakeholders must be **proactive** in the development, implementation and review of inclusive PE and SEN, and consult actively with each other. This would ensure the views and opinions of all stakeholders are considered in order to address the current issue of lack of coherence. This additionally compliments recommendations from the DfES

(2001a) to work together to create co-ordinated and coherent (Avramadis and Norwich 2002) provision through **partnership** and collaborative approaches. It is vital that we see the process of including children with SEN in PE as a holistic partnership and that we do not see ourselves as isolated figures in striving to meet the needs of particular individuals. Thus whilst we are all unique individuals, we are much stronger if we work together collectively towards our common goals.

Inclusive PE for children with SEN requires a recognition and commitment to modify, adapt, and change existing teaching, learning and assessment strategies, policies and practices in order to facilitate full access and entitlement to the curriculum (Ainscow 1999, Skrtic 1991). The development of inclusive PE must therefore be recognised as part of a **process** model that evolves, emerges and changes over time, and as such needs regular review by all stakeholders. Any process involves dynamic discussion and debate and a desire to learn from mistakes as well as celebrate successes.

In summary, all stakeholders must ensure inclusion is reflected within their **policy** documentation, as a means of monitoring, reviewing and evaluating delivery. This also seeks to publicly state how agencies are going to respond to inclusive practice, and can be used as a means of holding people to account (Depauw and Doll-Tepper 2000, Lloyd 2000). However, stakeholders must ultimately recognise the need to move policies through into the **pedagogical** practices of lecturers, trainee and qualified teachers, and school staff in order to ensure they have the necessary skills to deliver inclusive PE to children with SEN. Consequently, whilst philosophies and processes are vital they must in due course be measured in terms of effective and successful inclusive **practice** that values person-centred approaches to the education of children with SEN. This will only be achieved if you as an individual, and with colleagues, are honest and true to yourself in considering all eight aspects of the Eight P framework.

Task 9.1 The Eight P framework

Reflect upon the Eight P framework noted above and interpret what each of these statements means to you, and what action you need to take to ensure you embed these principles into your practice.

Let the children have their say

In interpreting the Eight P inclusive PE and SEN framework (Vickerman 2002) as a basis for determining the context for reflection and delivery of your practice, the next stage is to consider what else we need to know in order to enhance the knowledge and understanding which has been gained from this book. Dyson (2001) supports this view, suggesting 'there is an inevitable desire for unequivocal guidance on what to do next' (Dyson 2001: 28) and therefore it would be remiss of this book not to offer suggestions for future action and research related to inclusive PE for children with SEN.

Therefore, the next stage of any research or teaching and learning activity would be to focus upon hearing the voices of children with SEN in order to enhance current knowledge and understanding of inclusive PE. At present there is very little research or practical resource information that identifies the real value in working with and consulting the people that we serve – the children with SEN. It is hoped that in years to come there will be a wealth of good practice materials to share on this issue, but it would be remiss in this final chapter not to acknowledge the valuable role that consultation and engagement with pupils in teachers' understanding of children's specific needs has.

Depauw and Doll-Tepper (2000) suggest that 'successful inclusion requires decision-makers and individuals with a disability to have choice (informed choice) and to have choices' (Depauw and Doll-Tepper 2000: 139) with regard to the nature of their involvement in physical activity. In order to facilitate choice there is a need for agencies and individuals to work within a culture which offers a commitment to improve the expertise of teachers, and offer flexible learning and instructional environments to meet the individual needs of children with SEN (Hofman 2003).

Consequently, in gauging the views of children with SEN, Farrell (2000) indicates that an integral aspect of teachers and pupils having informed choice and decision-making is asking questions such as:

> What do pupils with SEN prefer, special or mainstream school? This is a potentially interesting and under researched area. What are pupils' reflections on the assessment process? Did they have choice in the provision they were offered? What changes would they like to see in their provision?
> (Farrell 2000: 157)

In examining questions and concepts of empowerment and consultation, Farrell's (2000) suggestions can be considered in keeping with existing social models of disability (Reiser and Mason 1990) which are grounded in beliefs that people (children and adults) should have opportunities to empower themselves – thus ensuring the views of children with SEN are considered

---

Task 9.2 Consultation

Reflect upon the quote from Farrell (2000) and ask yourself if the children you work with have been given genuine choice and opportunity to voice their views and opinions. If not then ask yourself the question why, and what you could do to address this issue?

fully in any planning, delivery, and evaluation of inclusive practice. Thus, the involvement of individuals and agencies should be to sought to avoid erecting barriers that might either block this process or disregard the vital role that they play in examining the inclusion process (Christensen and James 2000).

Pensgaard and Sorensen (2002) suggest, for example, that there is a great need to examine concepts of empowerment and offer guides to research with individuals with disabilities. Furthermore, they suggest, 'The role that perceived control plays in the lives of human beings is an important area of investigation within an empowerment perspective' (Pensgaard and Sorenson 2002: 55) and as a consequence should play a significant role in any interpretation or suggested models for the delivery of inclusive practice.

Hutzler *et al.* (2002) supports this view, linking the concepts of inclusion and empowerment, based on the belief that personal empowerment of children with disabilities is an integral component in helping to understand the inclusion process. In their study on examining the views and opinions of children with disabilities, for example, they found over half of the negative physical activity experiences of children with SEN attributed failure as due to a lack of empowerment. As a result, children with SEN advocated the use of consultation as a means of addressing this issue in the future, and authors such as Mayall (2000) suggest consultation and empowerment of children with SEN are important mechanisms in understanding the issues that matter to children.

Future directions

It is evident from the examination above that the establishment of mechanisms for consultation and empowerment is a vital ingredient to gaining a full appreciation of all the perspectives of inclusive PE for children with SEN. Therefore, the next logical steps in the progression and extension of work in the field of PE and SEN would be to move research and teaching, learning and assessment practice in this direction. In considering potential approaches to address this, the work undertaken by Goodwin and Watkinson (2000) regarding children with disabilities' descriptions of good days and bad days, and their involvement in inclusive PE, serves as a valuable starting point for future action – especially as it addresses many of the issues highlighted by the authors above in relation to consultation with and empowerment of children with SEN. Goodwin and Watkinson (2000) noted that children with SEN described good days in PE as being focused around having a sense of belonging, skilful participation and sharing in the benefits of engagement and participation in the lesson. In contrast, bad days were described as being focused around social isolation, competence being questioned and restricted participation. If we are genuinely to 'hear the voices of the children' then we must take note of these reflections by the pupils we serve.

Task 9.3 Children's different experiences
Use the table below to review what and why you think children have different PE experiences, and the range of strategies you could employ to address any points of concern whilst celebrating aspects of success.

Good days/bad days	What and why is the experience occurring?	What strategies can we employ to celebrate success, whilst identifying solutions to problems
Good days Experiencing a sense of belonging		
Good days Engaging in skilful participation		
Good days Sharing in the benefits of engagement and participation		
Bad days Focused around social isolation		
Bad days Competence being questioned		
Bad days Focused upon restricted participation and engagement		

Concluding thoughts

It is hoped that this book has offered you many opportunities to stimulate discussion, debate and reflection on your work with children with SEN in PE. Including children with SEN within mainstream education has grown rapidly over a fairly short period of time, and in the majority of cases the experience has been a positive one for children and teachers alike. What we need to do next is be prepared to seize opportunities and problems and challenge our practice, matched by a desire and commitment to adopt flexible teaching, learning and assessment approaches. If we are prepared to do this it will benefit all children – not just those with SEN. In conclusion, the involvement and consultation of children with SEN as part of their schooling cannot be better emphasised than through a quote from Luke Jackson (then aged 13, in his autobiography *Freaks, Geeks and Asperger Syndrome: A User Guide to Adolescence*):

> I used to have a teacher who helped me at school, but at the time I didn't have a clue what she helped me with . . . whatever level of understanding the child you are working with has got, then I reckon you should still try to involve the child so that they know what is going on.
>
> (Luke Jackson 2002: 115)

Task 9.4 Maintaining commitment

Reflect upon Luke Jackson's statement as a final thought in this book and ask yourself the question, how can I ensure that the comments made by him remain at the forefront of my personal teaching philosophy?

Further reading

1 The context for inclusion

British Association of Advisers and Lecturers in Physical Education (BAALPE) (soon to become part of the Association for Physical Education) website: http://www.baalpe.org/
This website offers useful links to PE documentation and information on including children with SEN, including practical strategies, safe practice and resource guides.

English Federation for Disability Sport (EFDS) website: http://www.efds.net/
This website offers a range of links to local, regional, national and international agencies involved in the promotion and development of disability sport. The website has many useful links and a dedicated research section which updates you on current initiatives and practices.

Fredrickson, N. and Cline, T. (2002), *Special Educational Needs, Inclusion and Diversity*, Open University Press, Birmingham
This book, although not PE specific, offers a detailed contextual overview of all aspects of SEN, inclusion and diversity. It will be useful as a resource for extended reading to this chapter.

Physical Education Association for the United Kingdom (PEA(UK)) (soon to become part of the Association of Physical Education) website: http://www.pea.uk.com/
This website offers useful links to PE documentation and information on including children with SEN, ranging from practical strategies, safe practice and resource guides.

2 Children with special educational needs

Ainscow, M., Farrell, D., Tweddle, D. and Malkin, G. (1999), *Effective Practice in Inclusion and in Special and Mainstream Schools Working Together*, HMSO, London
This text provides information on best practices in inclusion both in special and mainstream schools. The publication will be of use in extending your understanding of the core principles of ensuring children with SEN, teachers and the wider school community work effectively together.

Contact a Family (CAF Directory) http://www.cafamily.org.uk/
Contact a Family is the only UK-wide charity providing advice, information and support to the parents of all disabled children. It states that, across the UK, a child is diagnosed with a severe disability every 25 minutes and over 98 per cent of disabled children are cared for at home by a parent or other family member. This directory puts parents and those who support disabled children in touch with each other to offer mutual support and insight into children's specific needs.

Wright, H. and Sugden, D. (1999), *Physical Education for All – Developing Physical Education in the Curriculum for Pupils with Special Educational Needs*, David Fulton, London
This book offers an insight into specific issues of including children with SEN in PE. The book offers a series of general principles in addition to providing an overview of the range of needs that you may face when working with pupils with SEN.

3 Movement, learning and ranges of special educational need

Place, K. and Hodge, S. (2001), 'Social Inclusion of Students with Physical Disabilities in General Physical Education: A Behavioural Analysis', *Adapted Physical Activity Quarterly*, 18, 389–404
This research paper offers a useful insight into the inclusion of children with physical disabilities in PE. The paper offers a range of research and theoretical applications to support the study's findings. Any teacher who is involved in planning, delivering and evaluating inclusive PE should read this research paper as a starting point for understanding many of the issues and challenges that may occur.

Volger, E. and Romance, T. (2000), 'Including a Child with Severe Cerebral Palsy in Physical Education: A Case Study', *Adapted Physical Activity Quarterly*, 17, 161–182
This research paper gives insight into the access and entitlement to PE of children with cerebral palsy. The case study offers a clear insight into the challenges posed for teachers and pupils in ensuring they receive their entitlement to activity.

Winnick, J. (2000), *Adapted Physical Education and Sport*, (3rd edition), Human Kinetics, Leeds
This book provides a detailed overview of a wide range of disabilities and their associated characteristics. The book also gives a detailed account of teaching and learning strategies and begins to interpret what adapted PE actually consists of and what methods need to be employed to ensure the needs of children with SEN are met.

4 The Physical Education National Curriculum and inclusion

Auxter, D., Pyfer, J. and Hueltig, C. (2001), *Principles and Methods of Adapted Physical Education and Recreation* (9th edition), McGraw-Hill, New York
This book offers an insight into several key principles for adapting and modifying PE lessons. The book is a useful starting point to extend your reading on the methods and strategies you may wish to consider as part of the development of your teaching and learning activity with children with SEN.

Hutzler, Y., Fliess, O., Chacham, A. and Auweele, Y. (2002), 'Perspectives of Children with Physical Disabilities on Inclusion and Empowerment: Supporting and Limiting Factors', *Adapted Physical Activity Quarterly*, 19, 300–317
This research article offers an overview of the potential barriers to including children with SEN in physical activities. The article will help you to reflect upon some of the issues that can often be problematic with inclusive activity and will help you to take steps in advance to address these.

Vickerman, P., Hayes, S. and Wetherley, A. (2003), 'Special Educational Needs and National Curriculum Physical Education', in Hayes, S. and Stidder, G. (eds), *Equity in Physical Education*, Routledge, London
This book chapter offers a range of strategies for including children with SEN in PE.

5 Planning for and assessing children with SEN

Frapwell, A., Glass, C. and Pearce, L. (2002), 'Assessment "Work in Progress"', *The British Journal of Teaching Physical Education*, 33 (3): 23–25
This research paper offers an opportunity to review the context of assessment in PE and the related issues around the topic area.

Peach, S. and Bamforth, C. (2002), 'Tackling the Problems of Assessment, Recording and Reporting in Physical Education and Initial Teacher Training', *The British Journal of Teaching Physical Education*, 33 (2): 19–22
This paper focuses upon issues of preparing trainee teachers for the process of assessing, recording and reporting in PE. The paper focuses upon some of the issues and challenges that face ITT providers in ensuring trainee PE teachers are adequately prepared for the assessment process.

Piotrowski, S. (2000), 'Assessment, Recording and Reporting', in Bailey, R.P. and Macfadyen, T.M. (eds) *Teaching Physical Education 5–11*, Continuum, London.
This book chapter offers an insight into the process of assessment in PE, particularly within the primary phase. The book offers detailed definitions, interpretations and guidance on a range of assessment strategies and will be a useful resource for reflecting upon existing knowledge and understanding in PE.

6 Teaching and learning strategies

Christensen, P. and James, A. (2000), *Research with Children: Perspectives and Practices*, Falmer Press, London
This book offers an insight into methods of consultation and empowerment of children with SEN, from both a policy and a practice perspective. The book looks at the advantages and challenges, in consultation with young people, which will act as a point for reflection of your own teaching, learning and assessment style.

English Federation for Disability Sport (1999), *Including Disabled Pupils in Physical Education – Core Module*, EFDS, Manchester (www.efds.net/)
This resource pack offers core, primary and secondary modules in how to include children with SEN in PE lessons. The modules and booklet are based on practical strategies for developing inclusive activity and will help you to develop further the points raised within this chapter.

Norwich, B. (2002), 'Education, Inclusion and Individual Differences: Recognising and Resolving Dilemmas', *British Journal of Education Studies*, 50 (4): 482–502
This journal article offers an insight into the challenges that are posed in offering person-centred and individualised approaches to education. It looks at the tension between taking whole group approaches in contrast to individualised learning and is a useful prompt for further reflection and debate.

7 Multi-disciplinary approaches and working in partnership

Department for Education and Skills (2001), *Schools Achieving Success*, London, HMSO
This government document highlights examples of best practice related to schools identifying how they manage and achieve success. The document is of interest within the context of this chapter as it suggests that more partnership working is to be encouraged in order to share knowledge and understanding.

Lipsky, D. and Gartner, A. (1999), *Inclusion and Schools Reform: Transforming America's Classrooms*, Paul H. Brookes, Baltimore
This book focuses upon examining the transformation of inclusion within American schools and shares examples of practice on how reform has been achieved. One of the key features of the book is in identifying commitments to collaborative planning as a means towards achieving successful inclusion.

Rouse, M. and Florian, L. (1996), 'Effective Inclusive Schools: A Study in Two Countries', *Cambridge Journal of Education*, 26 (10): 71–85
This journal article offers an international comparison of indicators of effective inclusive schools. One of the central features that is identified within both case studies discussed in the paper is the need for individual agencies to work in partnership if inclusion is to function satisfactorily.

8 Opportunities outside the curriculum

Department for Education and Skills (2003), *Success for All: An Inclusive Approach to Physical Education and School Sport*, HMSO, London
This free CD-ROM resource offers teachers practical tips on how to include children with SEN in all six areas of activity in the PE curriculum. In addition it offers lots of resources and contacts for developing sporting opportunities for disabled children outside the formal school curriculum.

Goodwin, L. and Watkinson, J. (2000), 'Inclusive Physical Education from the Perspectives of Students with Physical Disabilities', *Adapted Physical Activity Quarterly*, 17, 144–160

This journal article looks at the views of children with SEN in relation to their inclusion in PE lessons. The article is of use in reflecting upon your current practices and how by having a greater appreciation of the needs of children with SEN we can then move on to developing their extra-curricular physical activity.

Sport England (1997), *Task Force on the Future of Disability Sport*, Sport England, London

This document provides in-depth background and context to the recommendations and action taken to address disability sport services for disabled children and adults. It will be useful in providing a historical overview to how provision has changed over recent years.

Youth Sport Trust: http://www.youthsporttrust.org/

The Youth Sport Trust is a charity established in 1994 to effect change and to build a brighter future for young people in sport. Integral to its core purposes is the inclusion of disable children, and they have established a series of resource cards and equipment bags to address this specific area.

9 Key principles for including children with SEN in PE

Goodwin, L. and Watkinson, J. (2000), 'Inclusive Physical Education from the Perspectives of Students with Physical Disabilities', *Adapted Physical Activity Quarterly*, 17, 144–160

This research paper picks up on and develops the concepts of good and bad days for children with SEN in PE. The article is worth reading as it is one of the few papers in circulation that has looked at the consultation of children and their views on the inclusion process.

Hofman, R. (2003), 'Staff Development and Commitment for a Successful Inclusion Policy', *International Journal of Inclusive Education*, 17 (2), 145–157

This journal article sets out to examine how schools can facilitate choice and work within a culture which offers a commitment to improve the expertise of teachers, and offer flexible learning and instructional environments. The central focus of the paper is on issues of staff development and looks at how teacher's professional practice can be developed with specific reference to SEN.

Jackson, L. (2002), *Freaks, Geeks and Asperger Syndrome: A User Guide to Adolescence*, Jessica Kingsley Publishers, London
This book offers a fascinating insight into the life and experiences of a young adolescent boy with Asperger's syndrome. Luke Jackson's personal reflections on his school experiences offer a real insight into his hopes, fears and points of celebration. It is a must-read for any teacher wishing to look at aspects of consultation and empowerment.

Bibliography

Ainscow, M. (1994), *Special Needs in the Classroom: A Teacher Education Guide*, Jessica Kingsley Publishers/UNESCO Publishing, London

Ainscow, M. (1995), 'Special Needs Through School Improvement: School Improvement Through Special Needs', in Clark, C., Dyson, A. and Millward, A. (eds), *Towards Inclusive Schools*, David Fulton, London

Ainscow, M. (1999), *Understanding the Development of Inclusive Schools*, Falmer Press, London

Ainscow, M. and Tweddle, D. (1998), *Encouraging Classroom Success*, David Fulton, London

Ainscow, M., Farrell, D., Tweddle, D. and Malkin, G. (1999), *Effective Practice in Inclusion and in Special and Mainstream Schools Working Together*, HMSO, London

Artiles, A. (1998), 'The Dilemma of Difference: Enriching the Disproportionality Discourse with Theory and Context', *Journal of Special Education*, 32 (1), 32–36

Audit Commission (2002), *Special Educational Needs: A Mainstream Issue*, HMSO, London

Auxter, D., Pyfer, J. and Hueltig, C. (2001), *Principles and Methods of Adapted Physical Education and Recreation* (9th edition), McGraw-Hill, New York

Avramidis, E. and Norwich, B. (2002), 'Teachers Attitudes Towards Integration/ Inclusion: A Review of the Literature', *European Journal of Special Needs Education*, 17 (2), 129–147

Bailey, R. (1999), 'Physical Education: Action, Play, Movement', in Riley, J. and Prentice, R. (eds), *The Primary Curriculum 7–11*, Chapman, London

Bailey, R. (2001), *Teaching Physical Education: A Handbook for Primary and Secondary Teachers*, Kogan Page, London

Ballard, K. (1997), 'Researching Disability and Inclusive Education: Participation, Construction and Interpretation', *International Journal of Inclusive Education*, 1 (3), 243–256

Barton, L. (1997), 'Inclusive Education: Romantic, Subversive or Realistic?' *International Journal of Inclusive Education*, 1 (30), 231–242

Barton, L. (ed) (1998), *The Politics of Special Educational Needs*, Falmer Press, London

Block, M. and Volger, E. (1994), 'Inclusion in Regular Physical Education: The Research Base', *Journal of Physical Education, Recreation and Dance*, 65 (1), 40–44

Booth, T. (1993), 'Raising Standards: Sticking to First Principles', in Dyson, A. and Gains, C. (eds), *Rethinking Special Needs in Mainstream Schools Towards the Year 2000*, David Fulton, London

Booth, T. (1995), 'Mapping Inclusion and Exclusion: Concepts for All?' in Clark, C., Dyson, A. and Millward, A. (eds), *Towards Inclusive Schools*, David Fulton, London

Booth, T., Ainscow, M. and Dyson, A. (1998), 'England: Inclusion and Exclusion, in a Competitive System', in Booth, T. and Ainscow, M. (eds), *From Them to Us: An International Study of Inclusion in England*, Routledge, London

Booth, T., Ainscow, M., Black-Hawkins, K., Vaughan, M. and Shaw, L. (2000), *Index for Inclusion: Developing Learning and Participation in Schools*, Centre for Studies on Inclusive Education, Bristol

British Association of Advisers and Lecturers in Physical Education (1989), *Physical Education for Children with Special Educational Needs in Mainstream Education*, White Line Publishing Services, Leeds

Bruner, J. (1971), *The Relevance of Education*, Norton, New York

Capel, S. (2001), *Learning to Teach Physical Education in the Secondary School*, Routledge, London

Capel, S. (2004), *Learning to Teach Physical Education in the Secondary School* (2nd edition), Routledge, London

Carroll, H. (1972), 'The Remedial Teaching of Reading: An Evaluation', *Remedial Education*, 7 (1), 10–15

Carroll, B. (1994), *Assessment in Physical Education: A Teacher's Guide to the Issues*, Falmer, London

Centre for Studies in Inclusive Education (2000), www.inclusion.uwe.ac.uk

Chambers, M. and Sugden, D. (2003), *Early Years Movement Skills: Description, Diagnosis and Intervention*, Whurr Publications, London

Cheminas, R. (2000), *Special Educational Needs for Newly Qualified and Student Teachers: A Practical Guide*, David Fulton, London

Christensen, P. and James, A. (2000), *Research with Children: Perspectives and Practices*, Falmer Press, London

Clark, C., Dyson, A. and Millward, A. (1995a), 'Towards Inclusive Schools: Mapping the Field', in Clark, C., Dyson, A. and Millward, A. (eds), *Towards Inclusive Schools*, David Fulton, London

Clark, C., Dyson, A., Millward, A. and Skidmore, D. (1995b), 'Dialectical Analysis, Special Needs and Schools as Organisations', in Clark, C., Dyson, A. and Millward, A. (eds), *Towards Inclusive Schools*, David Fulton, London

Clark, C., Dyson, A., Millward, A. and Skidmore, D. (1997), *New Directions in Special Needs: Innovations in Mainstream Schools*, Cassell, London

Clark, C., Dyson, A., Millward, A. and Robson, S. (1999), 'Theories of Inclusion, Theories of Schools: Deconstructing and Reconstructing the Inclusive School', *British Educational Research Journal*, 25 (2), 157–177

Collins, J. (1972), 'The Remedial Hoax', *Remedial Education*, 7 (3), 9–10

Corbett, J. and Slee, R. (2000), 'An International Conversation on Inclusive Education', in Armstrong, F., Armstrong, D. and Barton, L. (eds), *Inclusive Education: Policy Contexts and Comparative Perspectives*, David Fulton, London

Coupe, J. (1986), 'The Curriculum Intervention Model (CIM)', in Coupe, J. and Porter, J. (eds), *The Education of Children with Severe Learning Difficulties: Bridging the Gap Between Theory and Practice*, Croom Helm, London

Craft, D. (1996), 'A Focus on Inclusion in Physical Education', in Hennessy, B. (ed), *Physical Education Sourcebook*, Human Kinetics, Champaign

Croll, P. and Moses, M. (2000), 'Ideologies and Utopias: Education Professionals' Views of Inclusion', *European Journal of Special Needs Education*, 1–12

Daniels, H. and Garner, P. (1999), 'Introduction', in Daniels, H. and Garner, P. (eds), *World Yearbook of Education 1999: Inclusive Education*, Kogan Page, London

DCMS (Department for Culture, Media and Sport) (2002), *Game Plan: A Strategy for Delivering the Government's Sport and Physical Activity Objectives*, HMSO, London

DCMS/DfEE (Department for Culture, Media and Sport/Department for Education and Employment) (2001), *A Sporting Future for All: The Government's Plan for Sport*, HMSO, London

Depauw, K. and Doll-Tepper, G. (2000), 'Toward Progressive Inclusion and Acceptance: Myth or Reality? The Inclusion Debate and Bandwagon Discourse', *Adapted Physical Activity Quarterly*, 17, 135–143

Depauw, K. and Gavron, S. (1995), *Disability and Sport*, Human Kinetics, Champaign

DES (Department of Education and Science) (1978), *Special Educational Needs: Report of the Committee of Enquiry into the Education of Handicapped Children and Young People (The Warnock Report)*, HMSO, London

DES (Department of Education and Science) (1981), *The 1981 Education Act*, HMSO, London

DES (Department of Education and Science) (1984a), *Initial Teacher Training Approval of Courses*, Circular 3/84, HMSO, London

DES (Department of Education and Science) (1984b), *Initial Teacher Training Approval of Courses*, Circular 24/89, HMSO, London

DES (Department for Education and Science) (1989), *The Elton Report*, HMSO, London

DES (Department of Education and Science) (1992a), *Initial Teacher Training Approval of Courses*, Circular 9/92, HMSO, London

DES (Department of Education and Science) (1992b), *Physical Education in the National Curriculum*, London, HMSO

Dessent, T. (1987), *Making the Ordinary School Special*, Falmer Press, London

DfEE (Department for Education and Employment) (1997a), *Excellence for All Children: Meeting Special Educational Needs*, HMSO, London

DfEE (Department for Education and Employment) (1997b), *Initial Teacher Training Approval of Courses*, Circular 9/97, HMSO, London

DfEE (Department for Education and Employment) (1997c), *Teaching: High Status, High Standards – Requirements for Courses of Initial Teacher Training*, Circular 10/97, HMSO, London

DfEE (Department for Education and Employment) (1999), *Meeting Special Educational Needs: A Programme of Action – A Summary*, DFES Publications Centre, London

DfES (Department for Education and Skills) (1998a), *Teaching: High Status, High Standards – Requirements for Courses of Initial Teacher Training*, Circular 4/98, HMSO, London

DfES (Department for Education and Skills) (1998b), *Meeting Special Educational Needs: A Programme of Action*, DFES Publications Centre, London

DfES (Department for Education and Skills) (1998c), *SEN Excellence for All: Meeting Special Educational Needs*, HMSO, London

DfES (Department for Education and Skills) (2001a), *Schools Achieving Success*, London, HMSO

DfES (Department for Education and Skills) (2001b), *Special Educational Needs Code of Practice*, HMSO, London

DfES (Department for Education and Skills) (2001c), *Special Educational Needs and Disability Act*, HMSO, London

DfES (Department for Education and Skills) (2002a), *Education and Skills: Delivering Results – A Strategy to 2006*, HMSO, London

DfES (Department for Education and Skills) (2002b), *Healthy Living Blueprint for Schools*, HMSO, London

DfES (Department for Education and Skills) (2003), *Success for All: An Inclusive Approach to Physical Education and School Sport*, HMSO, London

DfES (Department for Education and Skills) (2004a), *Every Child Matters*, HMSO, London

DfES (Department for Education and Skills) (2004b), *Statistics of Education: Special Educational Needs in England, January 2000*, Circular 12/01, HMSO, London

DfES (Department for Education and Skills) (2005), *The English Green Paper for Youth (Youth Matters)*, HMSO, London

DfES/DCMS (Department for Education and Skills/Department for Culture, Media and Sport) (2002), *The Physical Education, School Sport, Club Links Strategy*, HMSO, London

DH (Department of Health) (2005), *Health Statistics*, HMSO, London

Disability Rights Task Force (1999), *From Exclusion to Inclusion*, HMSO, London

Disability Rights Task Force (2001), *Towards Inclusion: Civil Rights for Disabled People*, HMSO, London

Disability Rights Task Force (2003), www.drtf.org

DoE (Department of Education) (1870), *The Education for All Handicapped Children Act (1870)*, HMSO, London

DoE (Department of Education) (1944), *The Education Act (1944)*, HMSO, London

DoE (Department of Education) (1970), *The Education (Handicapped Act) 1970*, HMSO, London

DoE (Department of Education) (1988) *Education Reform Act*, HMSO, London

DoE (Department of Education) (1994) *Code of Practice on the Identification and Assessment of Special Educational Needs*, HMSO, London

Dunn, L. (1968), 'Special Education for the Mildly Retarded: Is much of it Justifiable?' *Exceptional Children*, 35, 5–22

Dyson, A. (1999), 'Issues of Inclusion', unpublished paper, Department of Education, University of Newcastle

Dyson, A. (2001), 'Special Needs in the Twenty-First Century: Where we've Been and Where we're Going', *British Journal of Special Education*, 28 (1), 24–29

Dyson, A. and Millward, A. (2000), *Issues of Innovation and Inclusion*, Paul Chapman, London

Dyson, A., Millward, A. and Skidmore, D. (1994), 'Beyond the Whole School Approach: An Emerging Model of Special Needs Practice and Provision in Mainstream Secondary Schools', *British Educational Research Journal*, 20 (3), 301–317

English Federation for Disability Sport (1999), *Including Disabled Pupils in Physical Education – Core Module*, EFDS, Manchester

English Sports Council (1997), *Disability Task Force Recommendations on the Future Structure and Integration of Disability Sport in England*, English Sports Council, London

Fairclough, S. and Stratton, G. (2005), 'Physical Activity Levels in Middle and High School Physical Education: A Review', *Paediatric Exercise Science*, 17, 217–236

Farrell, M. (1998), *The Special Education Handbook*, David Fulton, London

Farrell, P. (2000), 'The Impact of Research on Developments in Inclusive Education', *International Journal of Inclusive Education*, April, 153–164

Farrell, P. (2001), 'Special Education in the Last Twenty Years: Have things really got better?' *British Journal of Special Education*, 8 (1), 3–9

Feiler, A. and Gibson, H. (1999), 'Threats to the Inclusive Movement', *British Journal of Special Education*, 26 (3), 147–152

Frapwell, A., Glass, C. and Pearce, L. (2002), 'Assessment: Work in Progress', *British Journal of Teaching Physical Education*, 33, 23–25

Fredrickson, N. and Cline, T. (2002), *Special Educational Needs, Inclusion and Diversity*, Open University Press, Birmingham

Fuchs, D. and Fuchs, L. (1994), 'Inclusive Schools Movement and the Radicalisation of Special Education Reform', *Exceptional Children*, 60 (4), 294–309

Galloway, D. and Goodwin, C. (1979), *Educating Slow-Learning and Maladjusted Children: Integration or Segregation*, Longman, London

Gardiner, J. (1988) 'Functional Aspects of Re-collective Experience', *Memory and Cognition*, 16, 309–313

Giangreco, M., Dennis, R., Cloninger, C., Edelman, S. and Schattman, R. (1993), '"I've Counted Jon": Transformational Experiences of Teachers Educating Students with Disabilities', *Exceptional Children*, 59 (4), 359–372

Goodwin, L. and Watkinson, J. (2000), 'Inclusive Physical Education from the Perspectives of Students with Physical Disabilities', *Adapted Physical Activity Quarterly*, 17, 144–160

Haug, P. (1998), 'Norwegian Special Education: Development and Status', in Haug, P. and Tossebro, J. (eds), 'Theoretical Perspectives on Special Education, Norwegian Academic Press, Kristiansand

Henderson, S. and Sugden, D. (1992) *Movement Assessment Battery for Children*, Psychological Corporation, London

Her Majesty's Stationery Office (1998), *The Human Rights Act*, HMSO, London

Higher Education Funding Council for England (1984), *Assessment of the Quality of Education: Circular 3/93*, HEFCE, London

Hofman, R. (2003), 'Staff Development and Commitment for a Successful Inclusion Policy', *International Journal of Inclusive Education*, 17 (2), 145–157

Home Office (1995), *The Disability Discrimination Act*, HMSO, London

Hutzler, Y., Fliess, O., Chacham, A. and Auweele, Y. (2002), 'Perspectives of Children with Physical Disabilities on Inclusion and Empowerment: Supporting and Limiting Factors', *Adapted Physical Activity Quarterly*, 19, 300–317

Inner London Education Authority (1985), *Educational Opportunities for All?* (Fish Report), Inner London Education Authority, London

Ito, C. (1999) *Inclusion-Confusion*, www.wm.educ/ttac/articles/inclusion/htm

Jackson, L. (2002), *Freaks, Geeks and Asperger Syndrome: A User Guide to Adolescence*, Jessica Kingsley Publishers, London

Keogh, B., Gallimore, R. and Weisner, T. (1997), 'A Sociocultural Perspective on Learning and Learning Disabilities', *Learning Disabilities Research and Practice*, 12 (2), 107–113

Kolb, D. (1976) *The Learning Style Inventory*, McBer, Boston

Kyriacou, C. (1986), *Effective Teaching in Schools*, Blackwell, Oxford

Laban, R. (1942), *The Mastery of Movement* (4th edition), McDonald and Evans, London

Lipsky, D. and Gartner, A. (1999), *Inclusion and Schools Reform: Transforming America's Classrooms*, Paul H. Brookes, Baltimore

Lloyd, C. (2000), 'Excellence for all Children – False Promises! The Failure of Current Policy for Inclusive Education and Implications for Schooling in the 21st Century', *International Journal of Inclusive Education*, April, 133–152

Mayall, B. (2000), 'Conversations with Children: Working with Generational Issues', in Christensen, P. and James, A. (eds), *Research with Children: Perspectives and Practices*, Falmer Press, London

Mintzberg, H. (1979), *The Structuring of Organisations*, Prentice Hall, New York

Mintzberg, H. (1983), *Structure in Fives: Designing Effective Organisations*, Prentice Hall, New York

Mittler, P. (1985), 'Integration: The Shadow and the Substance', *Educational and Child Psychology*, 2 (3), 8–22

Moore, N. (2000), *How to do Research: The Complete Guide to Designing and Managing Research Projects* (3rd edition), Library Association Publishing, London

Mosston, M. and Ashworth, S. (1994), *Teaching Physical Education*, Macmillan, London

National Curriculum Council (1989), *Circular Number 5: Implementing the National Curriculum – Participation by Pupils with Special Educational Needs*, National Curriculum Council, York

Norwich, B. (1994), 'Differentiation from the Perspective of Resolving Tensions Between Basic Social Values and Assumptions about Individual Differences', *Curriculum Studies*, 2 (3), 289–308

Norwich, B. (2002a), 'Education, Inclusion and Individual Differences: Recognising and Resolving Dilemmas', *British Journal of Education Studies*, 50 (4), 482–502

Norwich, B. (2002b), *LEA Inclusion Trends in England 1997–2001: Statistics on School Placements and Pupils with Statements in Special Schools*, Centre for Studies on Inclusive Education, Bristol

OFSTED (Office for Standards in Education) (2000), *Secondary Physical Education: Main Findings*, OFSTED, London

OFSTED (Office for Standards in Education) (2002), *Handbook for the Inspection of Initial Teacher Training (2002–2008)*, OFSTED, London

OFSTED (Office for Standards in Education) (2003), *Inspecting Schools: Framework for Inspecting Schools Effective from September 2003*, OFSTED, London

Oliver, M. (1988), 'The Social and Political Context of Educational Policy: The Case of Special Needs', in Barton, L. (ed.), *The Politics of Special Educational Needs*, Falmer, London

Oliver, M. (1990), *The Politics of Disablement*, Macmillan, London

Peach, S. and Bamforth, C. (2002), 'Tackling the Problems of Assessment, Recording and Reporting in Physical Education Initial Teacher Training', *British Journal of Teaching Physical Education*, 33, 19–22

Pensgaard, A. and Sorensen, M. (2002), 'Empowerment Through the Sport Context: A Model to Guide Research for Individuals with Disability', *Adapted Physical Activity Quarterley*, 18, 48–67

Physical Education Association of the United Kingdom (2000) *Draft PEAUK Policy on Equal Opportunities*, unpublished report

Piaget, J. (1962), *Judgement and Reasoning in the Child*, Routledge, London

Pijl, S., Meijer, C. and Hegarty, S. (eds) (1997), *Inclusive Education: A Global Agenda*, Routledge, London

Piotrowski, S. (2000), 'Assessment Recording and Reporting', in Bailey, R. and MacFadyen, T. (eds), *Teaching Physical Education 5–11*, Continuum, London

Place, K. and Hodge, S. (2001), 'Social Inclusion of Students with Physical Disabilities in General Physical Education: A Behavioural Analysis', *Adapted Physical Activity Quarterly*, 18, 389–404

Porter, G. (1997), 'Critical Elements For Inclusive Schools', in Pijl, S., Meijer, C. and Hegarty, S. (eds), *Inclusive Education: A Global Agenda*, Routledge, London

Pring, R. (1996) 'Just Desert', in Furlong, J. and Smith, R. (eds) *The Role of Higher Education in Initial Teacher Training*, Kogan Page, London

QCA (Qualification Curriculum Authority) (1999a), *The National Curriculum for England: Physical Education Key Stages 1–4*, QCA, London

QCA (Qualification Curriculum Authority) (1999b), *The National Curriculum – Handbook for Primary Teachers in England*, QCA, London

QCA (Qualification Curriculum Authority) (1999c), *The National Curriculum – Handbook for Secondary Teachers in England*, QCA, London

QCA (Qualification Curriculum Authority) (2001), *Including All Learners: Key Principles to Guide QCA's Work*, QCA, London

QCA (Qualifications Curriculum Authority) (2003), www.qca.org.uk/menu.htm

Reiser, R. and Mason, M. (1990), *Disability Equality in the Classroom: A Human Rights Issue*, Inner London Education Authority, London

Reynolds, D., Teddlie, C., Hopkins, D. and Stringfield, S. (2000) 'Linking School Effectiveness and School Improvement', in Teddlie, C. and Reynolds, D. (eds), *The International Handbook of School Effectiveness Research*, Falmer Press, London

Richter, K., Adams-Mushett, C., Ferrara, M. and McCann, B. (1992), 'Integrated Swimming Classification: A Faulted System', *Adapted Physical Activity Quarterley*, 9, 5–13

Robson, C. (1999) *Real World Research: A Resource for Social Scientists and Practitioner Researchers*, Blackwell Publishers Ltd, Oxford

Rose, S. (1998) *Lifelines: Biology, Freedom, Determinism*, Penguin, London

Rouse, M. and Florian, L. (1996), 'Effective Inclusive Schools: A Study in Two Countries', *Cambridge Journal of Education*, 26 (10), 71–85

Rouse, M. and Florian, L. (1997), 'Inclusive Education in the Market Place', *International Journal of Inclusive Education*, 1 (4), 323–336

Sebba, J. and Sachdev, D. (1997), *What Works in Inclusive Education*, Barnardo's, Ilford

Sherrill, C. (1998), *Adapted Physical Activity, Recreation and Sport* (5th edition), McGraw Hill, Dubuque

Skrtic, T. (1991), 'The Special Education Paradox: Equity as the Way to Excellence', *Harvard Educational Review*, 61 (2), 148–206

Skrtic, T. (1995), 'The Functionalist View of Special Education and Disability: Deconstructing the Conventional Knowledge Tradition', in Skrtic, T. (ed.), *Disability and Democracy: Reconstructing (Special) Education for Post-modernity*, Teachers College Press, New York

Slininger, D., Sherrill, C. and Jankowski, C. (2000), 'Children's Attitudes Towards Peers with Severe Disabilities: Revisiting Contact Theory', *Adapted Physical Activity Quarterly*, 17, 176–198

Sport England (1997), *Task Force on the Future of Disability Sport*, Sport England, London

Sport England (1999), *Young People and Sport in England*, Sport England, London

Sport England (2001) *Disability Survey: 2000 Young People with a Disability and Sport: Headline Findings*, Sport England Publications, London

Sport England (2003), www.sportengland.org/resources/bibs/bibliogs.htm

Stilwell, J. and Wilgoose, C. (1997), *The Physical Education National Curriculum* (5th edition), Needham Heights, Allyn and Bacon

Sugden, D. and Henderson. S. (1994), 'Help with Movement', *Special Children*, 75, 1–8

Sugden, D. and Keogh, J. (1990), *Problems in Movement Skill Development*, University of South Carolina, Columbia

Sugden D. and Talbot, M. (1998), *Physical Education for Children with Special Needs in Mainstream Education*, Carnegie National Sports Development Centre, Leeds

Swann, W. (1985) 'Is the Integration of Children with Special Educational Needs Happening?' *Oxford Review of Education*, 11 (1), 3–18

Swann, W. (1988) 'Trends in Special School Placement to 1986: Measuring, Assessing and Explaining Segregation', *Oxford Review of Education*, 14 (2), 139–161

Swann, W. (1992) *Segregation Statistics*, London Centre for Studies on Integration, London

Tansley, A. and Guidford, R. (1960), *The Education of Slow Learning Children* (2nd edition), Routledge and Kegan Paul, London

Thomas, G., Walker, D. and Webb, J. (1998), *The Making of the Inclusive School*, Routledge, London

Tomlinson, S. (1982), *A Sociology of Special Education*, Routledge and Kegan Paul, London

Tomlinson, S. (1985), 'The Expansion of Special Education', *Oxford Review of Education*, 11 (2), 157–165

Trend, R. (1997) *Qualified Teacher Status: A Practical Introduction*, Letts Educational, London

TTA (Teacher Training Agency) (1997a), *Consultation on Standards for Special Educational Needs Co-ordinators*, Teacher Training Agency, London

TTA (Teacher Training Agency) (1997b), *Survey of Special Educational Needs Training Provided by Higher Education*, Teacher Training Agency, London

TTA (Teacher Training Agency) (1998a), *Framework for the Assessment of Quality and Standards in Teacher Training*, Circular 4/98, Teacher Training Agency, London

TTA (Teacher Training Agency) (1998b), *Survey of Special Educational Needs Training Provided by LEAs and National SEN Organisations*, Teacher Training Agency, London

TTA (Teacher Training Agency) (1999), *National Special Educational Needs Specialist Standards*, Teacher Training Agency, London

TTA (Teacher Training Agency) (2000), *Initial Teacher Training Performance Profiles: At a Glance (September)*, Teacher Training Agency, London

TTA (Teacher Training Agency) (2001a), *Handbook to Accompany the Standards for the Award of Qualified Teacher Status and Requirements for the Provision of Initial Teacher Training*, Teacher Training Agency, London

TTA (Teacher Training Agency) (2001b), *Standards for the Award of Qualified Teacher Status and Requirements for Initial Teacher Training: Consultation Document*, Teacher Training Agency, London

TTA (Teacher Training Agency) (2002), *Qualifying to Teach: Professional Standards for Qualified Teacher Status and Requirements for Initial Teacher Training*, Circular 02/02 (TTA 2002), Teacher Training Agency, London

TTA (Teacher Training Agency) (2003a), *Into Induction 2003: An Introduction for Trainee Teachers to the Induction Period for Newly Qualified Teachers*, Teacher Training Agency, London

TTA (Teacher Training Agency) (2003b), *The TTA Corporate Plan for 2003–2006*, TTA, London

TTA (Teacher Training Agency) and OFSTED (Office for Standards in Education) (2001), *Inspection Arrangements for Initial Teacher Training 2002/2003 Onwards: Consultation*, Teacher Training Agency, London

UCET (Universities Council for the Education of Teachers) (1997a), *Initial Teacher Education: TTA/OFSTED Quality Framework: A Critique. Occasional Paper Number 9, November*, UCET, London

UCET (Universities Council for the Education of Teachers) (1997b), *UCET Response to the Green Paper "Excellence for All Children"*, UCET, London

UNESCO (United Nations Educational, Scientific, and Cultural Organization) (1994), *The Salamanca Statement and Framework for Action on Special Needs Education*, Salamanca, UNESCO

United States of America Federal Government (1975), *Public Law 94–142, Education for All Handicapped Children*, US Federal Government, Washington DC

Vickerman, P. (1997), 'Knowing your Pupils and Planning for Different Needs', in Capel, S. *Learning to Teach Physical Education in the Secondary School*, Routledge, London

Vickerman, P. (2002), 'Perspectives on the Training of Physical Education Teachers for the Inclusion of Children with Special Educational Needs: Is There an Official Line View?' *Bulletin of Physical Education*, 38 (2), 79–98

Vickerman, P., Hayes, S. and Wetherley, A. (2003) 'Special Educational Needs and National Curriculum Physical Education', in Hayes, S. and Stidder, G. (eds), *Equity in Physical Education*, Routledge, London

Vincent, C., Evans, J., Lunt, I., Steedman, J. and Wedell, K. (1994), 'The Market Forces? The Effect of Local Management on Special Educational Needs Provision', *British Educational Research Journal*, 20 (3), 261–278

Vislie, L. and Langfeldt, G. (1996), 'Finance, Policy Making and the Organisation of Special Education', *Cambridge Journal of Education*, 26 (1), 59–70

Volger, E. and Romance, T. (2000), 'Including a Child with Severe Cerebral Palsy in Physical Education: A Case Study', *Adapted Physical Activity Quarterly*, 17, 161–182

Vygotsky, L. (1962), *Thought and Language*, MIT Press, Cambridge

Westwood, P. (1997), *Commonsense Methods for Children with Special Needs*, Routledge Press, London

Winnick, J. (1987), 'An Integration Continuum for Sport Participation', *Adapted Physical Activity Quarterly*, 4, 157–161

Winnick, J. (2000), *Adapted Physical Education and Sport* (3rd edition), Human Kinetics, Leeds

Wright, H. and Sugden, D. (1999), *Physical Education for All: Developing Physical Education in the Curriculum for Pupils with Special Educational Needs*, David Fulton, London

Index